Alpine
Beauty

Alpine and Subalpine Wildflowers
of the Canadian Rockies
and the Columbia Mountains

Neil L. Jennings

VICTORIA VANCOUVER CALGARY

Rocky Mountain Books   Rocky Mountain Books
#108 – 17665 66A Avenue   PO Box 468
Surrey, BC V3S 2A7   Custer, WA
www.rmbooks.com   98240-0468

Library and Archives Canada Cataloguing in Publication

Jennings, Neil L.
Alpine beauty: alpine and subalpine wildflowers of the Canadian Rockies and the Columbia Mountains / Neil L. Jennings.

Includes index.
ISBN 978-1-894765-83-1

1. Wild flowers—Rocky Mountains, Canadian (B.C. and Alta.)—Identification. 2. Wild flowers—British Columbia—Columbia Mountains—Identification. I. Title.

QK203.R63J46 2007   582.1309711   C2007-900009-6

Library of Congress Control Number:
2006940302

Edited by Corina Skavberg
Proofread by Joe Wilderson
Book design by John Luckhurst
Cover design by John Luckhurst
Front cover photo by Neil L. Jennings
All interior photos by Neil L. Jennings except as otherwise noted

Printed in Hong Kong

Rocky Mountain Books acknowledges the financial support for its publishing program from the Government of Canada through the Book Publishing Industry Development Program (BPIDP), and the province of British Columbia through the British Columbia Arts Council and the Book Publishing Tax Credit.

ACKNOWLEDGEMENTS

When I commenced work on this book, I was aware that
I would need assistance in obtaining photographs of many of the
included species. In that regard I contacted a number of wildflower
photographers who were known to me, and some who were perfect
strangers. Their generous support was heartening, and, indeed,
without it the project could not have been completed in the
timeframe desired. Particular thanks go to the photographers who
generously and graciously permitted me to use some of their work
in the book: Dennis Hall, Anne Elliott, Alan Youell, Cleve Wershler,
and Cliff Wallis of Calgary, Alberta; Russ Webb and Gill Ross of
Okotoks, Alberta; Glen Lee of Regina, Saskatchewan; and Lorna
Allen of Edmonton, Alberta. I also walked over a lot of country with
a wonderful and varied group of enthusiastic and knowledgeable
people who educated me about the wonders available for our
inspection. I wish to thank them for including me in the outings
that resulted in many of the photographs in the book. Special
mention goes to Dennis Hall, Anne Elliott, Russ Webb, Gill Ross,
Gillian Anderson, Wendy Agate, Anne Thompson, Helen Goudry,
Norma Lockwood, Homer and Elizabeth Spencer, Judy McPhee,
Ruth and Kent Goodwin, Laura and Jim Duncan, Susan Bond, Peter
Moody, and Shirley Hanson. I also want tip my hat to the Kimberley
Nature Park Society and its members, who selflessly, lovingly, and
generously tend to that marvelous piece of our world. Lastly, I want
to thank my wife, Linda, for her support, encouragement, patience,
and companionship in our past and future outings.

This book is dedicated to my wife, Linda, and my parents, Ken and Essie, whose unswerving support and affection have been the rock upon which all else is built.

CONTENTS

Introduction

This book is intended to be a guide for the amateur naturalist to the identification of wild flowering plants commonly found in the subalpine and alpine environments in the Rocky Mountains of western Canada. Those environments represent the "top of the world" in that geographical area, and the plants that exist there are generally different from those that exist at lower elevations. While there is some overlap, the differences are more dramatic at the higher elevations, owing in the main to the colder, wetter, and harsher conditions that prevail at higher elevations. The subalpine zone sits above the montane zone. As a general rule, the subalpine is divided into two sections—the lower subalpine and the upper subalpine. The lower subalpine zone tends to be a "dog hair" forest, with relatively thick conifer cover made up of subalpine fir, mountain hemlock, lodgepole pine, western larch, and Douglas fir predominant in the mix. The thick tree cover limits the light that reaches the forest floor, and shade tolerant vegetation is found there. Meadows, marshy areas and bogs are interspersed among the forest cover. As you move upward from the lower subalpine, there is a gradual shift to vegetation that is more adapted to shorter growing seasons and harsher winter conditions, including deeper snowpack. The upper subalpine zone tends to have more open forests, populated by subalpine fir, spruce, alpine larch, mountain hemlock, and lodgepole pine. Open grasslands and meadows become more frequent. The upper subalpine is cooler and wetter than the lower subalpine, with later snowfall, later snowmelt, and high winds being significant climatic conditions—all of which contribute to a shorter growing season.

The alpine zone lies above the upper subalpine, and it is characterized by the lack of tree cover. This zone is colder, more exposed to winds, and experiences heavy precipitation, particularly as snowfall. In this environment, low shrub and herb communities become the rule. The plants tend to be dwarf-sized, low-growing, fast-growing in the short season, prostrate, and hairy—all adaptations to the harsh environment.

The subalpine and alpine zones are like magnets to hikers and outdoor enthusiasts who visit the area. Encounters with wildflowers are, happily, inevitable and unavoidable when you are there, and recognizing the wildflowers will enrich the experience. It is my sincere belief that most people wish to know something about the flowers they see. "Do you know what this flower is called?" is one of the most often asked questions when I meet people in the field. Hopefully, the user will be able to answer the question by reference to the contents of this book. Identification of the unknown species is based on comparison of the unknown plant with the photographs contained in the book, augmented by the narrative descriptions associated with the species pictured in the book. In many cases the exact

species will be apparent, while in other cases the reader will be led to plants that are similar to the unknown plant, thus providing a starting point for further investigation. As a general rule, plant recognition is not hugely difficult, and I believe that most people will have a richer experience outdoors if they learn to recognize the wildflowers they encounter.

This book does not cover all of the species of wildflowers that exist in the subalpine and alpine zones, but it does cover the majority of the community that might be encountered in a typical day during the blooming season. Scientific jargon has been kept to a minimum. I have set out to produce the best photographic representations I could obtain, together with some information about the plant that the reader might find interesting, and that might assist the reader in remembering the names of the plants. This is not a book for scientists. It is a book for the curious. What I am attempting to do is assist people who want to be able to recognize and identify common wildflowers that they see while outdoors. I have tried to keep it simple, while making it interesting and enjoyable. In my view, what most people really want to know about wildflowers is "what is this thing?" and "tell me something interesting about it." Botanical detail, while interesting and enlightening to some of us, will turn off many people.

The plants depicted in the book are arranged first by colour, and then by family. This is a logical arrangement for the non-botanist because the first thing a person notes about a flower is its colour. All of the plants shown in the book are identified by their prevailing common names. Where I knew of other common names applied to any plant, I noted them. I have also included the scientific names of the plants. This inclusion is made to promote specificity. Common names vary significantly from one geographic area to another; scientific names do not. If you want to learn the scientific names of the plants to promote precision, fine. If you do not want to deal with that, fine. Just be mindful that many plants have different common names applied to them depending on geography and local usage.

A few cautionary comments and suggestions:

Go carefully among the plants so as not to damage or disturb them. In parks, stay on the established trails. In large measure, those trails exist to allow us to view the natural environment without trampling it to death. The environments at the top of the world are delicate and can be significantly damaged by indiscriminately tromping around in the flora.

Do not pick the flowers. Leave them for others to enjoy. Bear in mind that in national and provincial parks it is illegal to pick any flowers.

Do not attempt to transplant wild plants. Such attempts are most often doomed to failure.

Do not eat any plants or plant parts. To do so presents a potentially significant health hazard. Many of the plants are poisonous—some violently so.

Do not attempt to use any plants or plant parts for medicinal purposes. To do so presents a potentially significant health hazard. Many of the plants are poisonous—some violently so.

One final cautionary note—the pursuit of wildflowers can be addictive, though not hazardous to your health.

Neil L. Jennings
Calgary, Alberta

PLANT SHAPES AND FORMS

Parts of a Leaf

Parts of a Flower

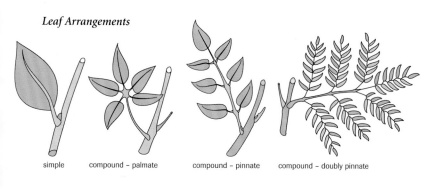

vein
midrib
blade
node
petiole

stamen { filament
anther
petal
sepal
stigma
style } pistil
ovary
receptacle
pedicel

Leaf Arrangements

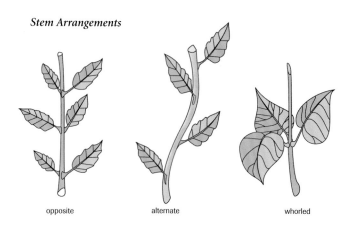

simple   compound – palmate   compound – pinnate   compound – doubly pinnate

Stem Arrangements

opposite   alternate   whorled

Leaf Shapes

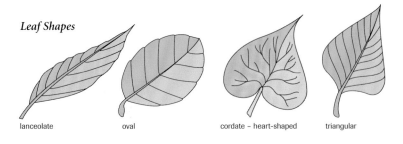

lanceolate   oval   cordate – heart-shaped   triangular

Leaf Margins

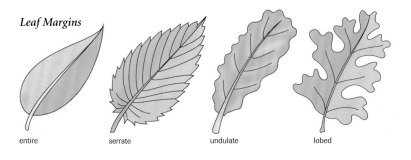

entire   serrate   undulate   lobed

Venation

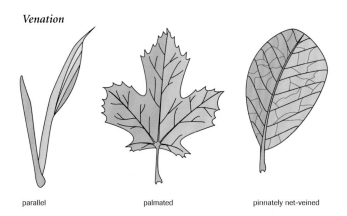

parallel   palmated   pinnately net-veined

TERRITORIAL RANGE OF WILDFLOWERS

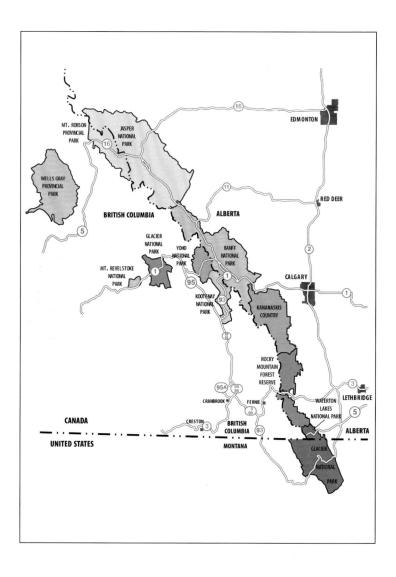

Blue and Purple Flowers

This section includes flowers that are predominantly blue or purple when encountered in the field—ranging from pale blue to deep purple, light violet to lavender. Some of the lighter colours of blue and purple might shade into pinks, so if you do not find the flower you are looking for here, check the other sections of this book.

Common Butterwort
Pinguicula vulgaris

BLADDERWORT FAMILY

This small plant is one of only a few carnivorous plants in the area.
It grows from fibrous roots in bogs, seeps, wetlands, stream banks, and
lakeshores, from valleys to the subalpine zone. The pale green to yellowish
leaves are basal, short-stalked, somewhat overlapping, curled in at the
margins, and form a rosette on the ground. The leaves have glandular hairs
on their upper surface that exude a sticky substance which attracts and then
ensnares small insects. The insects are then digested by the plant, enabling it
to obtain nitrogen and other nutrients. The flower is pale to dark purple,
solitary, and occurs atop a leafless stem.

The common name, Butterwort, is said to come from the buttery feel of
the leaves, *wort* being an Old English word that means "herb" or "a plant."
The genus name, *Pinguicula*, is the diminutive of the Latin word *pinguis*,
which means "fat," a reference to the soft, greasy-feeling leaves of the
plant.

Alpine Forget-Me-Not
Myosotis alpestris

BORAGE FAMILY

This beautiful, fragrant, little flower is easily recognized by its wheel-shaped blue corolla and its prominent yellow eye. This plant occurs, often in clumps, in moist subalpine and alpine meadows. The leaves are lance-shaped to linear. The lower leaves have short stems, but the upper ones are clasping. The stems are covered with long, soft hairs.

The genus name, *Myosotis*, is derived from the Greek *mus*, meaning "mouse," and *ous*, meaning "ear," descriptive of the furred leaves of some members of the genus. There seems to be some dispute as to the origin of the common name. One school of thought holds that the name dates back to the 1500s when tradition held that a blue flower was worn to retain a lover's affections. Another school of thought holds that a couple was walking along the Danube River, and the woman remarked on the beauty of some blue flowers blooming on a steep slope by the river. The man attempted to fetch the flowers for his sweetheart, but fell into the river, asking her, as he fell, to "forget me not." Alpine Forget-Me-Not is the state flower of Alaska.

Jones' Columbine

Aquilegia jonesii

BUTTERCUP FAMILY

Lorna Allen image

This beautiful dwarf Columbine is small, rare, grows on rocky, exposed slopes and limestone screes, and is said to be found in Canada only in Waterton Lakes National Park. The leaves are hairy, bluish-green, divided into small lobes, and occur in tufts near ground level. The flowers occur solitary on the stem, and appear disproportionately large for the size of the plant. The flowers are typical of Columbines, with 5 blue, wing-like sepals, and 5 blue, tube-shaped petals that flare at the open end and taper to a hooked spur at the other end. Numerous stamens and 5 pistils extend from the centre of the flower.

The origin of the genus name is discussed in the narrative on Yellow Columbine (*A. flavescens*), shown on page 121. This plant was originally collected by Charles Christopher Perry in 1873 in Wyoming, and the species name honours Captain W. A. Jones, who led an expedition into northwestern Wyoming in that year.

Low Larkspur
Delphinium bicolor
BUTTERCUP FAMILY

A plant of open woods, grasslands, and slopes, Larkspurs are easily recognized for their showy, highly modified flowers. The irregular petals are whitish to bluish, with sepals that are blue to violet. The upper sepal forms a large, hollow, nectar-producing spur. The flowers bloom up the stem in a loose, elongated cluster.

The genus name, *Delphinium*, is derived from the Greek word *delphin*, which means "dolphin," a reference to the plant's nectaries, which are said to resemble old pictures of dolphins. The common name is said to have originated because the spur on the flower resembles the spur on the foot of a lark. The flowers are favoured by bumblebees and butterflies. The plant contains delphinine, a toxic alkaloid, and is poisonous to cattle and humans.

Monkshood
Aconitum delphiniifolium

BUTTERCUP FAMILY

A plant of moist mixed coniferous forests and meadows, Monkshood has a distinctive flower construction that is unmistakable when encountered. The dark blue to purple flowers appear in terminal clusters, and the sepals form a hood, like those worn by monks.

The genus name, *Aconitum*, is derived from the Greek *acon*, meaning "dart," a reference to the fact that arrows were often tipped with poison from this plant, the entire plant being poisonous. The plant contains alkaloids that can cause paralysis, decreased blood pressure and temperature, and death within a few hours.

Dwarf Sawwort (Purple Hawkweed)
Saussurea nuda (also *S. densa*)

COMPOSITE FAMILY

Cleve Wershler image

This plant occurs on rocky slopes, ridges, and screes from moderate to high elevations, and stands up to 20 cm tall. When first encountered, it appears to be some sort of thistle. The leaves are alternate, hairy, lance-shaped, sharp-pointed, and crowded on the stem. The inflorescence is a dense, ball-like cluster on the end of the stem, from which protrude purple disk florets.

The genus name, *Saussurea*, honours Horace Benedict de Saussure, an 18th-century Swiss botanist, geologist, and alpinist. One of the species names, *nuda*, which means "naked," is puzzling. The other species name, *densa*, means "dense," and that makes much more sense, given the dense construction of the flower head.

Parry's Townsendia
Townsendia parryi

COMPOSITE FAMILY

This tap-rooted reddish-stemmed perennial blooms in the early spring, and appears on dry hills, stream banks, gravelly slopes, and grassy areas from prairie to alpine elevations. Most of the leaves are basal and form a rosette at ground level. The stems, leaves, and bracts are covered in white hairs. The relatively large flowers appear low to the ground on short stems, and they consist of broad ray flowers of violet to purple, surrounding bright yellow disk flowers.

The genus name, *Townsendia*, honours David Townsend, a 19th-century American botanist. The species name, *parryi*, honours Charles C. Parry, a 19th-century English naturalist and botanical explorer who came to America and catalogued a large number of plants. The Blackfoot boiled the roots of some Townsendias to make a concoction for treating ailments in horses. Another Townsendia occurs in the area, Low Townsendia (*T. hookeri*), but its ray flowers are white to pink, and the flowers are almost stemless.

Showy Aster
Aster conspicuus
COMPOSITE FAMILY

This plant is widespread and common in low to subalpine elevations, in moist to dry open forests, openings, clearings, and meadows. The flowers are few to many composite heads on glandular stalks, with 15–35 violet ray flowers, and yellow disk flowers. The stem leaves are egg-shaped to elliptical, with sharp toothed edges, and clasping bases.

Aster is the Latin name for "star," referring to the flower's shape. *Conspicuus* means "conspicuous," a reference to the showy flowers. Some Native peoples soaked the roots of the plant in water and used the liquid to treat boils. The leaves were also used as a poultice for that purpose.

Smooth Blue Aster

Aster laevis

COMPOSITE FAMILY

This plant inhabits open wooded areas, meadows, coulees, and ditches, often on gravelly soil. The plants are erect, up to 120 cm tall, and can form large colonies. The flowers are composed of pale to dark purple or bluish ray florets, surrounding bright yellow disk florets.

The genus name, *Aster*, is derived from the Latin for "star," a reference to the general shape of the flower. Smooth Blue Aster is believed to be a selenium absorber, and therefore dangerous to livestock who consume it. Selenium is a chemical element that is cumulative in the digestive system, and too much can lead to symptoms like the blind staggers.

Tall Purple Fleabane
Erigeron peregrinus

COMPOSITE FAMILY

This plant grows from a thick rootstock and can reach heights of 70 cm. It grows in the subalpine and alpine zones. The basal leaves are narrow and stemmed, while the stem leaves are smaller and stalkless. The flowers resemble daisies, with 30–80 rose- to purple-coloured ray florets, surrounding a yellow centre of disk florets. The large flowers are usually solitary, but there may be smaller flowers that appear from the axils of the upper leaves.

The origins of the common name, Fleabane, and the genus name, *Erigeron*, are discussed in the narrative on Daisy Fleabane (*E. compositus*), shown on page 48. This flower is sometimes referred to as Wandering Daisy.

Alpine Speedwell (Alpine Veronica)
Veronica wormskjoldii (also *V. alpina*)

FIGWORT FAMILY

This erect perennial stands up to 30 cm tall, and occurs in moist meadows and along streams in the subalpine and alpine zones. The leaves are elliptic to egg-shaped, and occur in opposite pairs, spaced along the stem. The stems, leaves, and stalks of the flowers are covered with fine, sticky hairs. The flowers are numerous and occur at the top of the stem. The corolla has 4 united blue petals, which exhibit dark veins.

The genus name, *Veronica*, honours Saint Veronica. According to the canonization, Veronica took pity on Jesus when he was carrying his cross to Golgotha (Calvary), and she used her kerchief to wipe sweat from his face. When the kerchief came back to her, it was impressed with an image of his face—the *vera iconica* or "true likeness." The sacred relic was kept in St. Peter's in the Vatican, but the name was applied to the genus to link Saint Veronica to a common flower often seen by the pious public. The species name, *wormskjoldii*, honours Morton Wormskjold, an 18th-century Danish naturalist. The common name, Speedwell, is said to come from the old English blessing or benediction "god speed," though why the name is applied to flowers of this genus is unknown.

Creeping Beardtongue
Penstemon ellipticus
FIGWORT FAMILY

One of the most handsome and conspicuous of the Penstemons, Creeping Beardtongue has large lavender-coloured flowers which seem out of proportion to the low growing plant. The plant grows in rocky crevices, taluses, and on cliffs in the subalpine and alpine regions. When in bloom, the flowers spill forth in amazing numbers, covering the leaves beneath in a blue-purple flood of colour.

The common name and genus name are explained in the note on Yellow Beardtongue (*P. confertus*), shown on page 134. The species name, *ellipticus,* refers to the leaves, which are egg-shaped or oblong, with rounded ends. In the springtime the beautiful flowers festoon rocky outcrops along trails. The plant is also known by the very appropriate common name Rockvine Beardtongue.

Kittentails
Besseya wyomingensis

FIGWORT FAMILY

Cliff Wallis image

This small plant is an early-bloomer, and is found in dry, open grasslands to subalpine rocky slopes. The leaves are mostly basal, oval to heart-shaped, toothed on the margins, and have long stalks. The stem has small, clasping leaves. The flowers are densely crowded in a spike atop the stem. The individual flowers consist of 2 or 3 green sepals, 2 purple stamens, and a purple style with a button-shaped stigma. There are no petals. The whole plant is covered in fine, white hairs.

The common name for the plant is said to be derived from the appearance of the inflorescence, with the purple stamens resembling a kitten's tail. The genus name, *Besseya*, honours Charles Bessey, a 19th-century American botanist. The reference in the specific name to Wyoming arises because the plant was first discovered in Wyoming. Indeed, a locally common name for the plant is Wyoming Kittentails.

Slender Beardtongue (Small-Flowered Penstemon)
Penstemon procerus

FIGWORT FAMILY

This plant grows to heights of 40 cm at low to alpine elevations, usually in dry to moist open forests, grassy clearings, meadows, and disturbed areas. Most of the blunt to lance-shaped leaves appear in opposite pairs up the stem. The flowers are small, funnel-shaped, blue to purple, and appear in one to several tight clusters arranged in whorls around the stem and at its tip.

The common name and genus name are explained in the note on Yellow Beardtongue (*P. confertus*), shown on page 134. The genus is a large and complex group of plants. There are dozens of Penstemons in the Rocky Mountains, and many will hybridize freely, adding even more confusion to the specific identification. This plant can usually be identified by its small, tightly packed blue flowers, which appear in whorls around the stem, often in interrupted clusters. The species name, *procerus*, is derived from Latin and means "very tall," which is somewhat peculiar because this plant is not usually very tall. Two other common names applied to the plant are Small-Flowered Penstemon and Small-Flowered Beardtongue.

Blue Flax
Linum perenne ssp. *lewisii*
FLAX FAMILY

A plant of dry, exposed hillsides, grasslands, roadsides, and gravelly river flats. The five-petaled flowers are pale purplish-blue, with darkish guidelines, yellowish at the base. The leaves are alternate, simple, and stalkless. The flowers appear on very slender stems that are constantly moving, even with the smallest of breezes.

The genus name, *Linum*, is derived from the Greek *linon*, meaning "thread." Each bud of this delicate flower blooms for only one day. The plant has been cultivated for various uses, notably oil and linen, since ancient times.

Mountain Gentian
Gentiana calycosa

GENTIAN FAMILY

Cliff Wallis image

This handsome flower appears in wet meadows and on stream banks in the subalpine and alpine zones. The leaves are opposite, egg-shaped, prominently veined, hairless, and smooth. The large flowers are funnel-shaped with 5 lobes, deep blue, and have conspicuous pleats between the petal lobes. The flowers are usually solitary, but as many as 3 might appear at the tip of the stem. Other flowers might appear in the axils of the upper leaves. Prior to opening, the petal tube displays a pointed spiral form, which has been compared to a swirled ice cream cone.

The genus name is discussed in the narrative associated with Northern Gentian (*Gentianella amarella*), shown on page 18. Plants in the genus *Gentiana* have pleats between the petal lobes, and lack the fringe inside the throat of the flower—both characteristics of the related genus *Gentianella*. There are two small alpine species of Gentians found in the area—Smooth Alpine Gentian (*G. glauca*) and Moss Gentian (*G. prostrata*). Smooth Alpine Gentian has dark blue to greenish-blue flowers that occur in a cluster at the terminal end of the stem. Moss Gentian has a creeping stem, pale green leaves with white margins, and a single blue to greenish-blue flower at the end of the stem.

Northern Gentian
Gentianella amarella (also *Gentiana amarella*)

GENTIAN FAMILY

A plant of moist places in meadows, woods, ditches, and stream banks, up to the subalpine zone. These lovely flowers are first sighted by their star-like formation winking at the top of the corolla tube, amidst adjacent grasses. The plant is most often small, standing only 15–20 cm, though taller specimens are sometimes seen. The flowers appear in clusters in the axils of the upper stem leaves, the leaves being opposite and appearing almost to be small hands holding up the flowers for inspection. There is a fringe inside the throat of the flower.

The genus name, *Gentianella*, comes from Gentius, a king of ancient Illyria, a coastal region on the Adriatic Sea. Gentius was said to have discovered medicinal properties in the plants of this genus. Gentians have been used as medicinal tonics for centuries. The species name, *amarella*, is derived from the Latin *amarus*, meaning "bitter," a reference to the bitter alkaloids contained in the plant's juices. The plant is also commonly referred to as Felwort. That name is derived from Old English *feld*, which means "field," and *wort*, which means "herb" or "a plant." Flowers in the genus *Gentianella* do not have pleats between the petal lobes. Flowers in the related genus *Gentiana* do have a pleat between the petal lobes and lack the fringe in the throat of the flower.

Smooth Alpine Gentian
Gentiana glauca

GENTIAN FAMILY

Lorna Allen image

This small perennial appears in subalpine and alpine meadows, growing in damp, stony places. The flower stems grow up to 10 cm tall, arising from a basal rosette of glossy, greenish-yellow leaves. Two or three pairs of opposite leaves appear on the upright stem. The flowers are greenish-blue, large considering the size of the plant, and occur in a tight cluster at the top of the stem. The corolla is tubular, with 4 or 5 lobes.

The origin of the genus name is discussed in the note on Northern Gentian (*Gentianella amarella*), shown on page 18. Another dwarf Gentian, the Moss Gentian (*G. prostrata*), appears in the same habitat. Moss Gentian has a creeping stem, pale green leaves with white margins, and a single blue to greenish-blue flower at the end of the stem.

Sticky Purple Geranium
Geranium viscosissimum

GERANIUM FAMILY

A plant of moist grasslands, open woods, and thickets. The plants can grow up to 60 cm tall. The flowers have large, showy, rose-purple to bluish petals, that are strongly veined with purple. The long-stalked leaves are deeply lobed, and split into 5–7 sharply toothed divisions, appearing in opposite pairs along the stem. There are sticky, glandular hairs covering the stems, leaves, and some flower parts. The fruit is an elongated, glandular hairy capsule, with a long beak, shaped like a stork's or crane's bill.

The genus name, *Geranium*, is derived from the Greek *geranos*, meaning "crane," a reference to the fruit being shaped like a crane's bill. Indeed, Crane's Bill is an oft-used common name for the Geraniums. The species name, *viscosissimum*, is the Latin superlative for *viscid*, which means "thick and gluey." The sticky, glandular hairs appearing on the stems and leaves effectively protect the plant from pollen theft by ants and other crawling insects. The Sticky Purple Geranium is very similar to a European import that has naturalized in dry grasslands in western North America—the Stork's Bill (*Erodium cicutarium*). Interestingly enough, *Erodium* is Greek for "heron," another bird with a long, pointed bill. The ornithological references to storks, herons, and cranes can certainly lead to some confusion when common names are applied to wildflowers of the Geranium Family.

Alpine Harebell
Campanula lasiocarpa

HAREBELL FAMILY

Lorna Allen image

This plant is the alpine version of the common Harebell. It grows on rocky slopes and screes high above timberline. The flower is quite large compared to the short stem and small leaves on the plant. The stem is seldom more than 10 cm tall, and it supports a single flower. The fruit is an oval, papery capsule that is covered with hairs.

The genus name, *Campanula*, is derived from the Latin *campana*, meaning "bell." *Campanula* is the diminutive of *campana*, thus "little bell." The species name, *lasiocarpa*, means "fuzzy fruit," a reference to the fruit of the plant.

Harebell
Campanula rotundifolia

HAREBELL FAMILY

This plant is widespread in a variety of habitats, including grasslands, gullies, moist forests, openings, clearings, and rocky open ground. The flowers are purplish-blue, rarely white, bell-shaped, with hairless sepals, nodding on a thin stem in loose clusters. The leaves are thin on the stem, and lance-shaped. The basal leaves are heart-shaped and coarsely toothed, but they usually wither before the flowers appear.

The origin of the genus name, *Campanula*, is explained in the note on Alpine Harebell (*C. lasiocarpa*), shown on page 21. The species name, *rotundifolia*, refers to the round basal leaves. This is the Bluebell of Scotland, and one school of thought holds that Harebell comes from a contraction of "heatherbell." Another school of thought holds that Harebell is a misspelling of "hairbell," the reference being to the hair-thin stems on which the flowers appear. Where Harebells occur, they can be in profusion, and can cast a purple hue to the area when they are in bloom. The Cree were said to have chopped and dried the roots to make into compresses for stopping bleeding and reducing swelling. The foliage contains alkaloids, and is avoided by browsing animals

Blue-Eyed Grass
Sisyrinchium montanum

IRIS FAMILY

These beautiful flowers are in the Iris Family, and can be found scattered among the grasses of moist meadows from the prairies to the subalpine zones. The distinctively flattened stems grow to heights of up to 30 cm, and are twice as tall as the grass-like basal leaves. The blue flower is star-shaped, with 3 virtually identical petals and sepals, each tipped with a minute point. There is a bright yellow eye in the centre of the flower. The blossoms are very short-lived, wilting usually within 1 day, to be replaced by fresh ones on the succeeding day.

The genus name, *Sisyrinchium*, was a name applied by Theophrastus, a disciple of Aristotle who refined the philosopher's work in botany and natural sciences in ancient Greece. It is a reference to a plant allied to the Iris. The species name, *montanum*, means "of the mountains," though, indeed, the plant is also found in other environments. The flower has a number of locally common names, including Montana Blue-Eyed Grass, Idaho Blue-Eyed Grass, Eyebright, Grass Widow, and Blue Star.

Blue Camas
Camassia quamash

LILY FAMILY

This plant of wet meadows and stream banks has long, narrow grass-like leaves, and a tall, naked stem. The startling blue to purplish flowers are numerous, and appear in a loose terminal cluster at the top of the stem. The flowers have 6 separate but similar petals and sepals that are spreading and somewhat unevenly spaced. The stamens are golden, and contrast vividly with the blue inflorescence of the plant.

The genus and species names for this plant are derived from the names given to the plant by the Nimi'-pu, or Nez Perce people. In September, 1805, Captain William Clark of the Lewis and Clark expedition, came upon some Nez Perce digging the bulbs of the plant for food. The Nez Perce shared the bulbs with the members of the expedition, at a time when food had grown scarce for the expedition. The onion-like bulbs were a very important food source for Native peoples, trappers, and settlers in western North America. The bulbs were baked, boiled, roasted, eaten raw, and ground into flour for baking bread. So important were the bulbs, that local wars were fought over the rights to certain large meadows where the plants grew in profusion. Victoria, British Columbia, was once called Camosun, meaning "a place for gathering camas." When the flowers are absent, Death Camas (*Zigadenus venenosus*), shown on page 73, and Blue Camas are very difficult to distinguish one from the other because the leaves and bulbs are very similar in appearance. This distinction can be deadly because the Death Camas is very poisonous, and deaths have been attributed to the failure to make the distinction.

Purple Onion (Wild Chives)
Allium schoenoprasum

LILY FAMILY

Allium is the Latin name for garlic and designates all wild onions. Wild Chives grow in wet meadows, along stream banks, in seeps, and at lake edges from low to subalpine elevations. The small pink or purple flowers are upright on the top of a leafless stalk and are arranged in a densely packed ball. Wild Chives have round hollow leaves near the base and produce a very distinctive "oniony" odour when broken.

Native peoples harvested wild onion bulbs before the plants flowered and used the bulbs as food, both raw and cooked. The bulbs were also used for flavouring other foods such as salmon and meat. Crushed onion bulbs were also used as a disinfectant and as a poultice to alleviate pain and swelling from insect bites. Garden chives are derived from this wild species.

Wild Mint (Canada Mint)
Mentha arvensis (also *Mentha canadensis*)
MINT FAMILY

This plant inhabits wetland marshes, moist woods, banks and shores of streams and lakes, and sometimes lives in shallow water. The purplish, to pinkish, to bluish flowers are crowded in dense clusters in the upper leaf axils. The leaves are opposite, prominently veined, and highly scented of mint if crushed. The stems are square in cross section, and hairy.

The genus name, *Mentha*, is from the Greek *Minthe*, a mythological nymph loved by Pluto. A jealous Proserpine changed the nymph into a mint plant. The species name, *arvensis*, means "growing in fields." The strong, distinctive taste of mint plants is from their volatile oils. The leaves have long been used fresh, dried, and frozen as a flavouring, and for teas. Some Native peoples used the leaves to flavour meat and pemmican, and lined dried meat containers with mint leaves prior to winter storage. Strong mint teas were used by Native peoples and European settlers as a treatment for coughs, colds, and fevers.

Bladder Locoweed (Inflated Oxytrope)
Oxytropis podocarpa
PEA FAMILY

This alpine plant grows high above timberline on gravelly slopes, from a stout taproot that produces a rosette of leaves that lie flat on the ground. The leaves are covered with silvery hairs, and consist of 11–23 short, linear leaflets. The flower stalks are leafless, and rise just above the leaves, terminating with 2 or 3 pale purple, pea-like flowers about 2 cm long. Each flower has a dark purple, hairy calyx, with a characteristic beaked keel, formed from the 2 lower fused petals. This beaked keel distinguishes members of this genus from those of the Milk Vetches (*Astragalus*). The fruits are inflated, egg-shaped pods, up to 3 cm long, that turn bright red to purple in the fall. A style remains attached to the pointed end of the pod.

The genus name, *Oxytropis*, is derived from the Greek *oxys*, which means "sharp," and *tropis*, which means "keel," a reference to the beaked keel on the flowers in this genus. The species name, *podocarpa*, means "stalked fruits," a reference to the inflated pods of the plant. *Oxytropis* is the genus that contains Locoweeds, and, indeed, this plant is sometimes referred to as Stalked-Pod Crazyweed. Plants of this genus contain poisonous alkaloids that can cause the blind staggers in animals that consume them, hence the reference to loco or crazy.

Silky Lupine
Lupinus sericeus

PEA FAMILY

A leafy, erect, tufted perennial with stout stems that appears in sandy to gravelly grasslands, open woods, and roadsides, often growing in dense clumps or bunches. The plant can reach heights of up to 80 cm. The flowers are showy in dense, long, terminal clusters, and display a variety of colours in blues and purples, occasionally white and yellow. Tremendous colour variation can occur, even in plants that are very close to each other. Flowers have a typical pea shape, with a strongly truncated keel and a pointed tip. The leaves of Lupines are very distinctive. They are palmately compound and alternate on the stem, with 5–9 very narrow leaflets that have silky hairs on both sides.

The genus name, *Lupinus*, is derived from the Latin *lupus*, meaning "wolf." That much appears to be accepted, but how this name came to be applied to this plant is open to contention. Perhaps the best explanation is that the plants were once thought (inaccurately) to be a devourer or robber of soil nutrients, hence a wolf. In fact, the root nodules of Lupines produce a nitrogen-fixing bacteria that actually tend to enrich poor soil. The species name, *sericeus*, is from the Latin *sericus*, meaning "silk," a reference to the soft, silky hairs that cover the plant. The fruits of Lupine contain an alkaloid, and may be poisonous to some livestock, particularly sheep.

Jacob's Ladder
Polemonium pulcherrimum

PHLOX FAMILY

Russ Webb image

This beautiful plant grows in dry, open, rocky environments in the montane to alpine zones. The leaves are distinctive. They are pinnately compound, with 11–25 round to elliptic leaflets that are evenly spaced to resemble a tiny ladder. The leaf arrangement gives the plant its common name—a reference to the story in the Book of Genesis wherein Jacob found a ladder to heaven. The pale to dark blue, cup-shaped flowers appear in an open cluster at the top of the stem. The flowers have a vivid orange ring at the base of the cup. The plant is covered with glandular hairs, which are said to impart the foul odour of the plant.

There are two schools of thought as to the origin of the genus name, *Polemonium*. One school holds that the name comes from the Greek philosopher Polemon. The other holds that the name is derived from the Greek word *polemos*, which means "strife." According to this school of thought, a dispute as to who discovered the plant, and its supposed medicinal properties, sparked a war between two kings! The species name is derived from the Latin *pulcher*, which means "beautiful" or "very handsome." The plant is apparently a favourite of bees.

Sky Pilot (Skunkweed)
Polemonium viscosum

PHLOX FAMILY

This beautiful plant is closely related to Jacob's Ladder, and is found in the alpine zone growing on exposed scree slopes. The leaves consist of numerous leaflets that are closely packed, short, whorled, and fern-like. The leaves are covered with sticky hairs, and have an odour of skunk, giving rise to one of the common names for the plant. The five-lobed blue flowers are funnel-shaped, and appear in clusters. Inside the flower there is a circle of yellow stamens, and a long, thread-like style.

The origin of the genus name is discussed in the narrative for Jacob's Ladder (*P. pulcherrimum*), shown on page 29. The species name, *viscosum*, is derived from the Latin *viscid*, which means "sticky or gluey," a reference to the sticky leaves of the plant. Surprisingly, given the odour of the leaves, the flowers of the plant are said to be sweet-scented.

Shooting Star
Dodecatheon pulchellum

PRIMROSE FAMILY

This beautiful plant is scattered and locally common at low to alpine elevations in warm, dry climates, grasslands, mountain meadows, and stream banks. The leaves appear in a basal rosette, and are lance to spatula-shaped. The flowers appear, one to several, nodding atop a leafless stalk. The flowers are purple to lavender, occasionally white, with corolla lobes turned backwards. The stamens are united into a yellow to orange tube, from which the style and anthers protrude.

A harbinger of spring, these lovely flowers bloom in huge numbers, and the grasslands take on a purple hue when the Shooting Stars are in bloom. The genus name, *Dodecatheon*, is derived from the Greek *dodeka*, meaning "twelve," and *theos*, meaning "gods," thus a plant that is protected by twelve gods. The species name, *pulchellum*, is Latin for "beautiful." Native peoples used an infusion from this plant as an eyewash, and some looked upon the plant as a charm to obtain wealth. Some tribes mashed the flowers to make a pink dye for their arrows. The common name is an apt description of the flower, with the turned back petals streaming behind the stamens.

Purple Saxifrage
Saxifraga oppositifolia
SAXIFRAGE FAMILY

Cliff Wallis image

This plant is a very low, matted plant, with tightly packed stems, common to the rocky talus slopes, ledges, and boulder fields in the alpine zone of the Rocky Mountains. The five-petaled purple flowers appear singly on short stems. The leaves are opposite, stalkless, and appear whorled. Each leaf is broadly wedge-shaped and bluish-green.

The genus name, *Saxifraga*, is derived from the Latin *saxum*, meaning "rock," and *frangere*, meaning "to break," a reference to the belief that plants in the genus are capable of breaking rocks into soil. The species name, *oppositifolia*, refers to the opposite arrangement of the leaves. Purple Saxifrage is the official flower of Nunavut.

Silky Phacelia (Silky Scorpionweed)
Phacelia sericea

WATERLEAF FAMILY

This plant grows on dry, rocky, open slopes at moderate to high elevations. The leaves are deeply divided into many segments and covered with silky hairs. The purple to blue flowers occur in clusters up a spike, resembling a bottle brush. The individual flowers are funnel-shaped, with long, purple, yellow-tipped stamens sticking out. The clusters of coiled branches resemble scorpion tails, thus the common name.

The genus name, *Phacelia*, is derived from the Greek *phakelos*, meaning "bundle," a reference to the dense flower clusters. The species name, *sericea*, means "silky," a reference to the fine hairs on the plant. Some people experience a dermatological reaction if they handle the plant.

White, Green, and Brown Flowers

This section includes flowers that are predominantly white or cream-coloured, green, or brown when encountered in the field. Given that some flowers fade to other colours as they age, if you do not find the flower you are looking for in this section, check the other sections in the book.

Sitka Alder

Alnus crispa

BIRCH FAMILY

This deciduous shrub grows up to 5 m tall, and is commonly found from low elevations to timberline in forests, clearings, and seepage areas. The leaves are broadly oval, with rounded bases, pointed tips, and double-toothed margins. The male and female flowers develop with the leaves. The male catkins are long and drooping; the female catkins are short and cone-like.

Native peoples made various uses of Sitka Alder, from basket making, to smoking fish and meat, to making a reddish dye. Alders improve soil fertility by fixing nitrogen in nodules on their roots.

Buckbrush Ceanothus (Snowbrush)

Ceanothus velutinus

BUCKTHORN FAMILY

This erect evergreen shrub grows to heights of up to 2 m on well-drained slopes in the montane and subalpine forests, and is abundant after a forest fire. The aromatic leaves are alternate and oval, finely toothed, dark green on the top, and greyish underneath. A varnish-like sticky substance covers the upper leaf surface, giving it a shiny appearance and a strong aroma. The leaves have 3 prominent veins that radiate from the leaf base. The flowers bloom in the early summer, and are tiny and white, heavily scented, and occur in dense clusters on reddish stalks at the ends of the branches.

The common name, Buckbrush, comes from the fact that deer and elk often browse on this plant in the winter. The leaves and stems of the plant contain a toxic glucoside—saponin—but ungulates seem to have no ill-effects from eating the plant. The seeds of the plant can survive in the soil for up to two centuries, and fire stimulates them to germinate. Young shrubs grow rapidly after a fire, but are eventually shaded out by trees.

Alpine Bistort (Viviparous Knotweed)
Polygonum viviparum

BUCKWHEAT FAMILY

Anne Elliott image

This plant grows up to 30 cm tall, and is found in moist meadows and along stream banks in the subalpine and alpine zones. The leaves are basal, lance-shaped, dark green, and shiny. The flowers are small, white (sometimes pink), and occur in a cluster at the top of an upright spike. The lower flowers give way to small purplish bulblets, each of which is capable of producing a new plant—whether dislodged from the stem or, indeed, still attached to the parent plant. These bulblets actually germinate while still attached to the parent plant.

The genus name, *Polygonum*, is derived from the Greek *poly*, meaning "many," and *gonu*, meaning "knee," a reference to the contorted rootstock from which the plant grows. The contorted shape of the rhizome may also be the source of the common name Knotweed. Some Native peoples viewed this root as snake-like in appearance, and that led some to believe that Bistort might be an anti-venom for snake bite. The species name, *viviparum*, is Latin meaning "producing or bringing forth live young," a reference to the bulblets of the plant. Some Native peoples used the roots and leaves as a food source.

Cushion Buckwheat (Silver-Plant)
Eriogonum ovalifolium
BUCKWHEAT FAMILY

This mat-forming species can be found from prairie elevations to the alpine ridges. The sometimes large mats of the plant are distinctive and appealing to the eye on high rocky ridges. The leaves are oval in shape, and densely covered in silver woolly hairs, giving the plant an overall grey or silver appearance. The white to cream-coloured flowers occur in dense, rounded heads atop short, leafless stems that arise from the basal growth. A plant may have numerous such flowering stems. The flower umbels in this species are simple, not compound as in most members of the genus.

The genus name, *Eriogonum*, is derived from the Greek *erion*, which means "wool," and *gonu*, which means "knee" or "joint," a reference to the woolly, jointed stems of many members of the genus. The flowers of this genus usually have an unpleasant smell, but the nectar appears to be relished by bees, and produces a strongly flavoured buckwheat-like honey.

Baneberry
Actaea rubra
BUTTERCUP FAMILY

A plant of moist shady woods and thickets, often found along streams. Baneberry is a tall, often branching, thick-stemmed, leafy perennial. The flower is a dense, white, cone-shaped cluster that appears on top of a spike. The fruit is a large cluster of either shiny red or white berries. At the time of flowering, there is no way to determine whether the berries of a particular plant will be red or white.

The common name of the plant is derived from the Anglo-Saxon word, *bana*, meaning "murderer" or "destroyer"—undoubtedly a reference to the fact that the leaves, roots, and berries of this plant are extremely poisonous. As few as 2 berries can induce vomiting, bloody diarrhea, and finally, cardiac arrest or respiratory paralysis. The genus name, *Actaea*, is derived from the Greek *aktaia*, meaning "elder tree," as the leaves are similar to elder leaves. The species name, *rubra*, is Latin for "red," a reference to the berries. There have been reports of children who have died as a result of eating the berries.

Globeflower
Trollius albiflorus
Buttercup Family

This plant grows from thick rootstock and fibrous roots, and is found in moist meadows, along stream banks, and in open, damp areas in the subalpine and alpine zones. The mostly basal leaves are shiny, bright green, palmately divided into 5–7 parts, and deeply toothed. The stem leaves are few, alternate, and short-stalked. The flowers are made up of 5–10 white sepals (which may have a pinkish tint on the outside) that surround a central core filled with numerous dark yellow stamens.

There seems to be some confusion among the learned authorities as to the origin of the genus name, *Trollius*. The most likely resolution is that the genus name is a Latinized version of the Swiss-German common name, *trollblume*, which means "troll flower." The reference to troll, a malevolent supernatural being, probably arises because this plant contains a poisonous alkaloid. Just prior to opening, and during inclement weather, the flower head appears round, thus the common name Globeflower. Globeflower might be confused with Mountain Marsh Marigold (*Caltha leptosepala*), shown on page 41, where they co-exist. The leaves of Mountain Marsh Marigold are heart-shaped, not oblong, and not divided into segments, as are those of Globeflower.

Mountain Marsh Marigold
Caltha leptosepala
Buttercup Family

Gill Ross image

This plant lives in marshes, on stream banks, and in seeps in the subalpine and alpine zones. The leaves are mostly basal, simple, long-stemmed, oblong to blunt arrowhead-shaped, with wavy or round-toothed margins. The flowers are solitary on the end of the stem, and consist of 5–12 petal-like sepals that are white, tinged with blue on the back. The flower has a bright yellow centre, composed of numerous stamens and pistils.

The genus name, *Caltha*, is derived from the Greek *kalathos*, which means "goblet," most probably a reference to the shape of the open flower. The species name, *leptosepala*, is derived from the Greek *lepto*, which means "thin or narrow," and *sepala*, referring to the sepals. This plant contains glucosides which are poisonous. Mountain Marsh Marigold might be confused with Globeflower (*Trollius albiflorus*), shown on page 40, which grows in similar habitat. The flowers are similar, but the leaves on Globeflower are deeply divided and sharply toothed.

Northern Anemone
Anemone parviflora

BUTTERCUP FAMILY

Also known as Few Flowered Anemone, this plant prefers moist soils and streamside habitats in the subalpine and alpine areas. The stalk stands up to 30 cm, and supports a single flower with 5 or 6 creamy white, hairy sepals. On the stem below the flower there is a ring of 3 deeply cleft leaves.

The genus name, *Anemone*, is most probably derived from the Greek *anemo*, meaning "wind," a reference to the fact that the seeds of members of the genus are distributed by the wind. These flowers are also referred to as Wood Anemones.

Western Anemone (Chalice Flower)
Pulsatilla occidentalis (also *Anemone occidentalis*)

BUTTERCUP FAMILY

This plant is considered by many to be characteristic of wet alpine meadows and clearings. The large, creamy-white flowers bloom early in the spring, as the leaves are beginning to emerge. The entire plant is covered with hairs, which keep it protected in its cold habitat. Most of the leaves are basal, but there is a ring of feathery, grey-green stem leaves just below the flower. The flower is replaced by a clumped top of plumed seeds at the tip of the flowering stem. These seed clusters have been variously referred to as "mops," "shaggy heads," and "blond wigs," and give rise to another common name, Towhead Babies.

The common name, Chalice Flower, refers to the cup-shape inflorescence of the plant. A more recently coined name that has found some favour is Hippie On A Stick, a reference to the seed pod of the plant.

Cow Parsnip
Heracleum lanatum

CARROT FAMILY

A plant of shaded riverine habitat, stream banks, and moist open aspen woods, this plant can attain heights of over 2 m. The flowers are distinctive, with their large, compound, umbrella-shaped clusters (umbels) composed of numerous white flowers, with white petals in fives. The leaves are compound in threes, usually very large, softly hairy, deeply lobed, and toothed.

Heracleum refers to Hercules, likely because of the plant's large size. Cow Parsnip is also locally known as Indian Celery and Indian Rhubarb. The roots were cooked and eaten by some Native peoples, though there are some sources that say they are poisonous. The Blackfoot roasted the young spring stalks and ate them. They also used the stalks in their Sun Dance ceremony. Caution should be taken to distinguish this plant from the violently poisonous Water Hemlock (*Cicuta maculata*).

Mountain Sweet-Cicely
Osmorhiza chilensis

CARROT FAMILY

This member of the Carrot Family prefers moist to wet, shady habitat, and grows up to a metre in height. The leaves are twice divided into 3 parts, and are deeply cleft and toothed. The flowers are inconspicuous, and occur in white to greenish compound, umbrella-shaped clusters. The fruits of the plants in this genus have short beaks that often cling to the fur of passing animals, or the clothing of passing hikers.

The genus name, *Osmorhiza*, is derived from the Greek *osme*, meaning "scent," and *rhiza*, meaning "root," a reference to the sweet licorice odour given off by the plant's roots and fruits when they are crushed. Many Native peoples used the roots as a food source, and also for a variety of medicinal purposes. Some tribes held the plant sacred, and prohibited all but holy men from touching it.

Sharptooth Angelica (Lyall's Angelica)
Angelica arguta

CARROT FAMILY

A plant of shaded riverine habitat, stream banks, and moist open woods, this plant can attain heights of over 2 m. The numerous white flowers are arranged in compound umbels. The leaves are twice compound, with large leaflets that are sharply toothed, as is reflected in the common name for the plant. The lateral leaf veins are directed to the ends of the teeth on the leaf margin. The very poisonous Water Hemlock (*Cicuta maculata*), has similar flowers, and should not be confused with Sharptooth Angelica. In Water Hemlock the leaf veins are directed to the notch between the teeth on the leaf margin.

The genus name, *Angelica*, is derived from the Latin *angelus*, meaning "angel." There appear to be several schools of thought as to how this reference to angels arose. One school of thought has it that a revelation was made by an angel to Matthaeus Sylvaticus, a 14th-century physician who compiled a dictionary of medical recipes of the beneficial medicinal properties of the plant. Another school of thought is that the flower usually blooms near in time to the celebration of the feast of St. Michael the Archangel. The species name, *arguta*, is Latin, meaning "sharp toothed." The other common name, Lyall's Angelica, is in honour of David Lyall, a Scottish botanist and geologist who collected specimens while working on the boundary survey between Canada and the United States in the 1880s. Angelicas are highly prized by herbalists for treating digestive disorders.

Hooker's Thistle
Cirsium hookerianum

COMPOSITE FAMILY

This thistle can grow up to a metre tall and is found in a variety of habitats, from valleys up to alpine elevations. The flower heads are white, and the bracts surrounding the flowers point upward. The leaves, stems, and bracts are all covered with silky hairs. The leaves display a prominent midvein.

The genus name, *Cirsium*, is derived from the Greek *kirsos*, meaning "swollen vein," a reference to a once-held belief that members of this genus could remedy that physical problem. The species name, *hookerianum*, celebrates Sir William Hooker, a prestigious English botanist who wrote extensively on the subject, and was the director of the Kew Herbarium and Botanical Garden in England during the second half of the 19th century. This plant was a source of food for some Native peoples, eaten either raw or cooked.

Daisy Fleabane
Erigeron compositus

COMPOSITE FAMILY

This daisy-like flower is one of several Fleabanes that occur in the subalpine and alpine zones. The leaves of this species are almost all basal, and are deeply divided. The leaves and the flowering stems are sparsely covered with short, glandular hairs. The flowers appear solitary at the top of the stem, and they are typical of flowers in the Composite Family—composed of ray flowers surrounding disk flowers. The ray flowers are numerous, and may be white, pink, or mauve. The disk flowers are numerous and yellow. The involucral bracts are hairy and purplish at the tips.

The genus name, *Erigeron*, is derived from the Greek *eri*, which means "spring," and *geron*, which means "old man," a reference to the hairy-tufted fruits of plants in the genus, or, perhaps, to the overall hairiness of many species in the genus. The species name, *compositus*, means "well-arranged," probably in reference to the neat appearance of the inflorescence. The common name, Fleabane, arises because it was once thought that bundles of these flowers brought into the house would repel fleas. Fleabanes and Asters are often confused. Fleabanes generally have narrower, more numerous ray florets than Asters. In addition, if you check the involucral bract—the small green cup under the flower—and see that all of the bracts are the same length, then you have a Fleabane. If some of the bracts are obviously shorter, you have an Aster.

Mountain Fleabane
Erigeron humilis

COMPOSITE FAMILY

This is one of several Fleabanes that occur in the subalpine and alpine zones. In this species, the leaves are basal, spoon-shaped, and taper into long stems. Long hairs cover all green portions of the plant. The hairs on the involucral bracts and upper stem are woolly and blackish-purple. The flowers appear solitary at the top of the short stem, and are typical of flowers in the Composite Family—composed of ray flowers surrounding disk flowers. The ray flowers are very numerous, thin, and white. The ray flowers often grow to be a light purple with age. The disk flowers are numerous and yellow.

The origins of the common name, Fleabane, and the genus name, *Erigeron*, are discussed in the narrative on Daisy Fleabane (*E. compositus*), shown on page 48. This plant is also called by the common name Purple Daisy.

Yarrow
Achillea millefolium
COMPOSITE FAMILY

A plant of dry to moist grasslands, open riverine forests, aspen woods, and disturbed areas. The individual white flower heads appear in a dense, flat-topped or rounded terminal cluster. The ray florets are white to cream-coloured (sometimes pink), and the central disk florets are straw-coloured. The leaves are woolly, greyish to blue-green, and finely divided, almost appearing to be a fern. Yarrow can occur in large colonies.

The common name is derived from the name of a Scottish parish. The genus name, *Achillea*, is in honour of Achilles, the Greek warrior with the vulnerable heel, who was said to have made an ointment from this plant to heal the wounds of his soldiers during the siege of Troy. The species name, *millefolium*, means "thousand leaves," in reference to the many finely divided leaf segments. Yarrow contains an alkaloid called achillean that reduces the clotting time of blood. It appears a number of Native peoples were aware of this characteristic of the plant, and made a mash of the crushed leaves to wrap around wounds.

Northern Black Currant (Skunk Currant)
Ribes hudsonianum

CURRANT FAMILY

An erect, deciduous shrub, growing up to 2 m tall at low to mid elevations in moist to wet forests. This plant does not have thorns, but does have yellow resin glands dotting its smooth bark. The leaves are alternate, maple-leaf-shaped with three to five rounded lobes. The flowers are white and saucer-shaped, and occur in spreading to erect clusters. The flowers have a strong smell that some people find objectionable. The fruits are black, speckled with resin dots, and said to have a particularly bitter taste.

Berries of all currants are high in pectin and can make excellent jams and jellies, though the raw berries are often insipid.

Sticky Currant
Ribes viscosissimum

CURRANT FAMILY

This plant is a shrub that grows up to 2 m high in damp woods and openings, from valleys to subalpine elevations. It does not have the prickles of many gooseberries and currants. The flowers are bell-shaped, yellowish-white, and often tinged in pink. The flowers and leaves are covered in glandular hairs that are sticky to the touch. The fruits are blue-black, sticky, and not considered edible.

The species name, *viscosissimum*, is derived from the Latin *viscosus*, meaning "sticky" or "viscid." The first known botanical specimen was collected by Meriwether Lewis in Idaho in 1806. Lewis' note on the plant in his journal says that the fruit is "indifferent & gummy."

Bunchberry (Dwarf Dogwood)
Cornus canadensis
DOGWOOD FAMILY

A plant of moist coniferous woods, often found on rotting logs and stumps. The flowers are clusters of inconspicuous greenish-white flowers, set among 4 white, petal-like, showy bracts. The leaves are in a terminal whorl of 4–7, all prominently veined. The leaves are dark green above, lighter underneath. The fruits are bright red berries.

The genus name, *Cornus*, is Latin for "horn" or "antler," possibly a reference to the hard wood of some members of this genus. Another school of thought is that the inflorescence of the plant bears a resemblance to the cornice piece, a knob on cylinders used for rolling up manuscripts. *Canadensis* is a reference to Canada, this plant being widely distributed across the country in the boreal forests. Bunchberry's common name is probably derived from the fact that the fruits are all bunched together in a terminal cluster. A Nootka legend has it that the Bunchberry arose from the blood of a woman marooned in a cedar tree by her jealous husband. The plant is reported to have an explosive pollination mechanism wherein the petals of the mature but unopened flower buds suddenly reflex and the anthers spring out, casting pollen loads into the air. When an insect brushes against the tiny bristle at the end of one petal, it triggers this explosion.

Red Osier Dogwood
Cornus stolonifera

DOGWOOD FAMILY

This willow-like shrub, which grows up to 3 m high, often forms impenetrable thickets along streams and in moist forests. The reddish bark is quite distinctive, and it becomes even redder with the advent of frosts. The leaves are heavily veined, dark green above and pale underneath. The flowers are small, greenish-white, and occur in a flat-topped cluster at the terminal ends of stems. The fruits are small white berries, appearing in clumps.

The common name, Osier, appears to be from the Old French *osiere*, meaning "that which grows in an osier-bed (streambed)." Native peoples used the branches of the plant to fashion fish traps, poles, and salmon stretchers. This plant is extremely important winter browse for moose.

Eyebright
Euphrasia arctica

FIGWORT FAMILY

These beautiful plants are tiny, standing only 10–15 cm tall. The leaves are sessile (stalkless), egg-shaped, sparsely hairy, glandular, and have decidedly toothed margins. The upper leaves are reduced in size, and the lovely white flowers appear there. The corolla is white with a hood-shaped upper lip. The lower lip is three-lobed and pencilled with violet. There are also yellow hues inside the tiny flowers.

A number of Eyebrights occur in the world, mostly in northern latitudes. The sample shown here was photographed in the Nordic Tracks above the town of Kimberley, British Columbia. At the time the plant was photographed in the summer of 2004, it appeared to be unknown to local botany enthusiasts. It has since been discovered in several locations in the general area.

Parrot's Beak
Pedicularis racemosa

FIGWORT FAMILY

This lovely plant favours upper montane and subalpine environments. The white flower has a very distinctive shape that deserves close examination to appreciate its intricacy. The flowers appear along a purplish stem that grows up to 35 cm tall. The fern-like leaves are simple, lance-shaped to linear, and have distinctive fine sharp teeth on the margins.

The origin of the genus name, *Pedicularis*, is explained in the narrative on Bracted Lousewort (*P. bracteosa*), shown on page 133. Parrot's Beak takes its common name from the long, slender downward turned beak on the upper lip of the petals. Another common name, Sickletop Lousewort, is a reference to the shape of the flowers. Another, similar species occurs in the area, the Contorted Lousewort (*P. contorta*), but usually at higher elevations.

White Geranium
Geranium richardsonii
GERANIUM FAMILY

A plant of moist grasslands, open woods, and thickets, this plant is very similar to Sticky Purple Geranium (*G. viscosissimum*), shown on page 20, except it has white to pinkish flowers with purple veins. The petals have long hairs at the base. The leaves are not sticky, and are hairy only along the veins of the lower sides of the leaves. The fruits are like those of the Sticky Purple Geranium, that is, capsules with long beaks, shaped like a crane's or stork's bill.

The fruit capsules are said to open explosively, with the beak splitting lengthwise from the bottom and catapulting the seeds away from the parent plant. White Geraniums seem to prefer partially shaded growing locations, rich in humus. The species name, *richardsonii*, is in honour of Sir John Richardson, a 19th-century Scottish botanist assigned to Sir John Franklin's expedition to the Arctic in search of the Northwest Passage.

Devil's Club
Oplopanax horridum
GINSENG FAMILY

If there were a contest for the meanest plant in the woods, this one would almost certainly qualify. The Devil's Club is aptly named. It has club-shaped woody stems that grow to over 2 m in height, and the stems are covered in stiff, sharp spines. The leaves are large, shaped like very large maple leaves, with sharp spines on their veins and leaf stalks, and sharp teeth on their margins. The flowers are small, white, and globe-shaped, and are arranged along a central flower stalk up to 25 cm long. The fruits are a mass of shiny red berries.

The genus name, *Oplopanax*, is derived from the Greek *hoplon*, meaning "weapon." The species name, *horridum,* comes from the same root as "horrible." The spines of the plant easily break off in skin, and the punctures occasioned will quickly become sore and inflamed. In spite of all this, the plant is quite handsome and regal. It also has a number of medicinal properties, and has been used by Native peoples and herbalists to treat such diverse ailments as arthritis, diabetes, cataracts, and indigestion. It is recommended that this plant be given a good inspection, but do not get too close.

Fringed Grass-of-Parnassus
Parnassia fimbriata

GRASS-OF-PARNASSUS FAMILY

These plants abound in riverine habitat, pond edges, and boggy places from montane to the subalpine zone. The white flowers are very delicate looking. The flowers appear as singles on a slender stem, with 5 white petals, and greenish or yellowish veins. The lower edges of the petals are fringed with hairs. Alternating fertile and sterile stamens are characteristic of this genus. The leaves are mostly basal and broadly kidney-shaped. A single leaf clasps the flowering stem about halfway up.

The name of this plant seems to present some confusion. One school of thought is that the genus name, *Parnassia*, is from Mount Parnassus in Greece, said to be a favourite retreat of the god Apollo. Another school of thought holds that the name comes from a description of the plant written in the 1st century by Dioscorides, a military physician for the Emperor Nero. When the description was translated, "grass" was included in the translation, and it stuck. There is no doubt that this plant is not even remotely grass-like. A similar species, Northern Grass-of-Parnassus (*P. palustris*) occurs in the same habitat, but it does not have the fringed margins of Fringed Grass-of-Parnassus.

Greenish Flowered Wintergreen
Pyrola chlorantha

HEATH FAMILY

An erect perennial that inhabits moist to dry coniferous and mixed forests, and riverine environments, from the montane to the subalpine zones. The flowers have 5 greenish-white, waxy petals, and a long style attached to a prominent ovary. The flowers have a bell shape and are distributed on short stalks up the main stem. The leaves are basal, in a rosette. The leaves have a leathery appearance and are shiny, rounded, and dark green.

The genus name, *Pyrola*, is derived from Latin *pyrus*, which means "a pear," probably a reference to the leaves being pear-shaped. Wintergreen leaves contain acids that are effective in treating skin irritations. Mashed leaves of *Pyrola* species have traditionally been used by herbalists in skin salves, and poultices for snake and insect bites. They are called wintergreen, not because of the taste, but because the leaves remain green during the winter. Like orchids, these plants require a specific fungus in the soil to grow successfully, and transplantation should not be attempted. Another species of *Pyrola*, Pink Wintergreen, (*P. asarifolia*), shown on page 177, is similar in shape and occurs in similar habitat, but has pink flowers.

Labrador Tea
Ledum groenlandicum

HEATH FAMILY

This evergreen, much-branched shrub is widespread in low to subalpine elevations in peaty wetlands and moist coniferous forests. The flowers are white and numerous, with 5–10 protruding stamens in umbrella-like clusters at the ends of branches. The leaves are alternate and narrow, with edges rolled under. They are deep green and leathery on top, with dense rusty hairs underneath.

The leaves, used fresh or dried, can be brewed into an aromatic tea, but should be used in moderation to avoid drowsiness. Excessive doses are reported to act as a strong diuretic. The aromatic leaves were used in barns to drive away mice, and in houses to keep away fleas.

One-Sided Wintergreen
Pyrola secunda (also *Orthilia secunda*)

GEATH FAMILY

A small forest dweller that grows to 5–15 cm tall. The white to yellowish-green flowers lie on one side of the arching stalk, arranged in a raceme of 6–10 flowers, sometimes more. The flowers resemble small street lights strung along a curving pole. The straight style sticks out beyond the petals, with a flat, five-lobed stigma. The leaves are basal, egg-shaped, and finely toothed at the margins.

One-Sided Wintergreen is included in the *Pyrola* genus by some taxonomists, but is put into the *Orthilia* genus by others. *Orthilia* is derived from the Greek *orthos*, meaning "straight," most probably a reference to the straight style. The species name, *secunda*, is derived from the Latin *secundus*, meaning "next" or "following," a reference to the flowers which follow each other on the same side of the stem. Once seen, this delightful little flower is unmistakable in the woods.

Oval-Leaved Blueberry
Vaccinium ovalifolium

GEATH FAMILY

This deciduous shrub grows to heights of over 2 m in low to subalpine elevations in moist to wet coniferous forests, clearings, and bogs. The pale pink flowers are urn-shaped, and appear singly at the leaf bases. The flowers may precede the arrival of the leaves. The berries are blue-black, dusted with a pale bluish bloom. The berries are somewhat large for wild blueberries, and have a pleasant flavour. The leaves are oval, blunt, and rounded at the ends, and usually lack teeth on the margins.

The genus *Vaccinium* includes all of the wild Blueberries, Cranberries, and Huckleberries. The species name, *ovalifolium*, refers to the shape of the leaves. Another common name applied to this plant is Blue Huckleberry.

Single Delight

Moneses uniflora (also *Pyrola uniflora*)

HEATH FAMILY

This delightful little forest dweller is also known as One Flowered Wintergreen, and it inhabits damp forests, usually on rotting wood. The plant is quite tiny, standing only 10 cm tall, and the single white flower, open and nodding at the top of the stem, is less than 5 cm in diametre. The flower looks like a small white umbrella, offering shade. The leaves are basal, oval, and evergreen, attached to the base of the stem. The style is prominent and tipped with a five-lobed stigma, which almost looks like a mechanical part of some kind.

The genus name, *Moneses*, is derived from the Greek *monos*, meaning "solitary," and *hesia*, meaning "delight," a reference to the delightful single flower. Other common names include Wood Nymph and Shy Maiden. In Greek mythology, nymphs were nature goddesses, beautiful maidens living in rivers, woods, and mountains, and once you see this diminutive flower, the common names seem completely appropriate.

White Heather (White Mountain Heather)
Cassiope mertensiana
HEATH FAMILY

This matting plant occurs in the subalpine and alpine zones. The flowers are white, bell-shaped and nodding at the end of the stems. The leaves are opposite, evergreen, and pressed so closely to the stems that the stems are all but hidden. The foliage forms low mats on the ground.

The genus name, *Cassiope*, is from Greek mythology. Cassiopeia was the wife of Cepheus, the King of the Ethiopians. She was vain and boastful, claiming that her beauty exceeded that of the sea nymphs. This claim offended and angered the sea nymphs, and they prevailed upon Poseidon, the God of the Sea, to send a sea monster to punish Cassiopeia by ravaging the land. In order to save the kingdom, the Ethiopians offered Cassiopeia's daughter, Andromeda, as a sacrifice, chaining her to a rock. Perseus, the Greek hero who slew the Gorgon Medusa, intervened at the last minute to free Andromeda and slay the monster. In astronomy, the constellation Perseus stands between Cassiopeia and Andromeda, still defending her today. While interesting, what all that has to do with this flower is a mystery. The species name, *mertensiana*, honours F.C. Mertens, an early German botanist. In fact, White Mountain Heather is not a heather at all, but a heath.

White Rhododendron
Rhododendron albiflorum

HEATH FAMILY

An erect and spreading deciduous shrub that grows up to 2 m high, and inhabits cool, damp woods, often establishing dense communities under the conifer canopy. The leaves are oblong to lance-shaped, and are covered with fine rusty-coloured hairs. The leaves turn to beautiful shades of crimson and orange in the fall. The flowers are large (up to 3 cm across), white, and cup-shaped, and are borne singly or in small clusters around the stem of the previous year's growth. The petals are joined to each other for about half of their length, and there are 10 stamens visible inside the flower. The flowers are deciduous, and fall off of the plant as a whole, often littering the forest floor with what appear to be intact flowers.

The genus name, *Rhododendron*, is derived from the Greek *rhodon*, meaning "rose," and *dendron*, meaning "tree." The species name, *albiflorum*, means "white-flowered." This plant is often referred to as Mountain Misery because it grows in dense communities, with branches trailing downhill, making it difficult for hikers to move through it. All parts of the plant contain poisonous alkaloids which are toxic to humans and livestock.

Black Elderberry
Sambucus racemosa

HONEYSUCKLE FAMILY

This is a tall deciduous shrub that grows to heights of several metres, occurring from low to subalpine elevations along streams, in moist thickets and clearings, and in shady forests. The opposite, branching stems of the plant are woody, stout, and filled with pith in the centre. The leaves are pinnately compound, with 5–7 leaflets that are pointed, lance-shaped, and sharply toothed. The flowers are white to creamy in colour, and occur in large pyramid-shaped clusters. The flowers have a relatively strong unpleasant odour. The fruits are black or purplish-black berries that appear in the late summer.

The fruits of this plant have long been used as a food source. Wine and jellies can be produced from the berries. Bears and birds seem quite partial to the fruits. The branches of the plant have been hollowed out to make whistles, drinking straws, pipe stems, and blowguns, but that practice is discouraged because the branches of the plant contain glycosides and are poisonous. Two other Elderberries occur in the same range—Blue Elderberry (*S. cerulea*), which has waxy, blue fruits, and Red Elderberry (*S. racemosa* var. *arborescens*), which has red fruits.

Low-Bush Cranberry (Mooseberry)
Viburnum edule

HONEYSUCKLE FAMILY

This plant is a sprawling deciduous shrub that grows to heights of up to
2 m, from low to subalpine elevations in moist to wet forests, along streams,
and in boggy areas. The leaves are opposite, sharply toothed, and maple-leaf
shaped with 3 lobes. The tiny, white, five-parted flowers appear in flat-
topped showy clusters between leaves along the stem. The fruits are clusters
of red or orange berries that contain a large, flattened stone. The fruits
remain on the plant after the leaves fall, and the over-ripe berries and
decaying leaves often produce a musty odour in the woods near the plants.

The species name, *edule*, means "edible," and refers to the fruits of the plant.
The fruits are favoured by birds. The fruits were used extensively by Native
peoples as a food source, and other parts of the plant were used medicinally.
In the fall, the leaves of this plant turn to beautiful crimson and purple
colours. Two other locally common names for the plant are Mooseberry and
Squashberry. Some confusion can arise because of the existence of a plant
called a High-Bush Cranberry (*V. trilobum*), which occurs in similar habitat.
That plant is a larger bush—almost a small tree—with similar flowers and
fruits. Neither the Low-Bush or the High-Bush are truly Cranberries, which
are members of the Heath Family. There is another plant in the area that is a
Cranberry—the Bog Cranberry (*Vaccinium oxycoccus*), shown on page 171.

Utah Honeysuckle (Red Twinberry)
Lonicera utahensis

HONEYSUCKLE FAMILY

This erect deciduous shrub grows up to 2 m tall. The leaves are opposite, elliptical to oblong, with smooth edges and blunt tips. The creamy-white flowers are trumpet-shaped and appear in pairs on a single stalk from the leaf axils. The fruits are red berries that are joined at the base.

Some Native peoples ate the berries of Utah Honeysuckle, which were said to be a good emergency source of water because the berries are so juicy. The flowers are frequented by hummingbirds. The plant is also known as Red Twinberry.

Beargrass
Xerophyllum tenax

LILY FAMILY

Gill Ross image

These impressive plants are common on dry hillsides and subalpine meadows in Waterton Lakes National Park, the only place in Alberta where they are found. They are also found in a variety of locations in southeastern British Columbia. The plant has a basal clump of dense, sharp leaves, from which rises an impressive stem. The flowers are a torch-shaped cluster of hundreds of small, white miniature lilies, which bloom first from the bottom of the cluster, and then work their way upwards. Individual plants may be sterile for several years, producing flowers only 1–3 times in a decade.

Some authorities attribute the common name Beargrass to the fact that bears have been reported to eat the leaves in the spring, but my research has led me to a different conclusion. The plant was first collected for science by Meriwether Lewis in 1806 in what is now the state of Idaho. At the time of the collection, Lewis believed the plant to be a kind of Yucca (*Yucca glauca*), a plant that was known to Lewis by one of its common names, "bear grass." Beargrass has some resemblance to Yucca, but Yucca grows in more arid environments at lower elevations. Even though Lewis was mistaken about this plant being a type of Yucca, the name Beargrass stuck. Native peoples are reported to have used the leaves for weaving exquisite baskets, capes, and hats. Various wild animals feed on various parts of the plant.

Bronzebells
Stenanthium occidentale

LILY FAMILY

This lily of moist woods, stream banks, meadows, and slopes has grass-like leaves that emerge from an onion-like bulb. The bell-shaped flowers are greenish-white, flecked with purple, and have 6 sharply pointed tips that twist backward, exposing the interior of the blossom. Ten or more graceful and fragrant flowers are hung along the length of the stem, drooping down.

The genus name, *Stenanthium*, is derived from the Greek *steno*, meaning "narrow," and *anthos*, meaning "flower." The appropriateness of this name will be testified to by any photographer who has tried to photograph this species in even a slight breeze. The species name, *occidentale*, means "western." Without question, this flower is extraordinarily attractive in its detail.

Clasping-Leaved Twisted-Stalk
Streptopus amplexifolius
LILY FAMILY

This member of the Lily Family grows in moist, shaded forests, and has a widely branching zigzag stem, with numerous sharply pointed, parallel-veined leaves that encircle the stem at each angular bend. The plant varies in height from 30–100 cm. The glossy leaves often conceal the small, pale white or greenish flowers that dangle on curving, thread-like stalks from the axil of each of the upper leaves. In fact, one can walk by the plant without noticing the flowers hiding under the leaves. The flowers have strongly reflexed petals and sepals, and appear to be hanging on the plant like small spiders dangling on fine webs. The fruits of the plant are very handsome orangish-red oval berries.

The genus name, *Streptopus*, is derived from the Greek *streptos*, meaning "twisted," and *pous*, meaning "foot," referring to the twisted flower stalks. The species name, *amplexifolius*, is derived from the Latin *amplexor*, meaning "to surround," and *folius*, meaning "a leaf."

Death Camas
Zigadenus venenosus

LILY FAMILY

This plant of moist grasslands, grassy slopes, and open woods grows from an onion-like bulb that has no oniony smell. The leaves are mainly basal, and resemble grass, with prominent midveins.The greenish-white, foul-smelling flowers appear in tight clusters atop an erect stem, each flower having 3 virtually identical petals and sepals. There are yellowish-green V-shaped glands (nectaries) near the base of the petals and sepals.

The genus name, *Zigadenus*, is derived from the Greek *zygos*, meaning "yoke," and *aden*, meaning "gland," a reference to the shape of the nectary at the base of each petal and sepal. The species name, *venenosus*, is Latin for "very poisonous." Death Camas contains poisonous alkaloids, and is probably even more toxic than its close relative, White Camas (*Z. elegans*), shown on page 82, which appears in the same general habitat, but blooms later. These plants have been responsible for killing many people and animals. When the flowers are missing, Death Camas and White Camas are difficult to distinguish from Blue Camas (*Camassia quamash*), another lily, the bulb of which was commonly used as a food source by Native peoples and early settlers.

Fairybells
Disporum trachycarpum
LILY FAMILY

A plant of shaded poplar woods, stream banks, and riverine environments, this delightful flower blooms in early summer. The flowers are bell-shaped, creamy white, and occur in drooping pairs at the end of branches. The leaves of the plant are generally lance-shaped with pointed ends. The fruits are red egg-shaped berries, occurring in pairs.

The genus name, *Disporum*, is derived from the Greek *dis*, meaning "double," and *spora*, meaning "seeds." The species name, *trachycarpum*, means "rough fruited." The berries from Fairybells are edible, but said to be bland. They are a favoured food of many rodents and birds.

False Solomon's Seal
Smilacina racemosa

LILY FAMILY

A lily of moist woods, river and stream banks, thickets and meadows, that can grow up to half a metre tall. The flowers are small and white, arranged in a branching panicle that is upright at the end of the stem. The leaves are broadly lance-shaped, numerous and alternate, gradually tapering to a pointed tip, with prominent parallel veining, sometimes folded at the midline. The fruit is a red berry flecked with maroon.

The genus name, *Smilacina*, means "a small Smilax," and refers to this plant's resemblance to plants in the genus *Smilax*. The species name, *racemosa*, indicates that the plant has a raceme arrangement for the flowers. This name is somewhat confusing, in that a raceme is an unbranched cluster of flowers on a common stalk. The flower arrangement on this plant is more precisely referred to as a panicle—a branched flower cluster that blooms from the bottom up. A very similar plant lives in the same habitat—the Star Flowered Solomon's Seal (*S. stellata*), but it has significantly fewer flowers, which are shaped like six-sided stars.

Indian Hellebore (False Hellebore)
Veratrum viride

LILY FAMILY

A tall, stout, often fuzzy-haired perennial with many leaves that inhabits moist forests, thickets, bogs, wet meadows, and avalanche chutes. The greenish flowers are somewhat inconspicuous and occur in long, open, drooping clusters along a substantial stalk that arises from the centre of the generally basal leaves. The stamens are yellow-tipped. Perhaps the most distinctive feature of this robust plant is the leaves. They are large, dull green, with long, closed sheaths at the base. Each leaf is broadly elliptic with a pointed tip, and has a prominently veined or ribbed smooth surface above, and a hairy underside. The basal leaves appear well before the flowers, and seem to whirl up from the earth, dwarfing all other plants around them.

This plant is also known as Green False Hellebore, a reference apparently to the genus name, *Veratrum*, being used in ancient time to apply to a true hellebore, which was a member of the Helleborus Family. The genus name is derived from the Latin words *vere*, meaning "true," and *atrum*, meaning "black," a reference to the black roots of the true hellebore. The species name, *viride*, means "green." This plant contains very toxic alkaloids which can cause symptoms similar to heart attacks. People have died from eating it, and, indeed, the Blackfoot are said to have used the plant to commit suicide. The plant is most dangerous early in the growing season, and is said to have caused accidental poisonings among cattle and sheep. Early American settlers boiled the roots and combed the resulting liquid through their hair to kill lice.

Queen's Cup
Clintonia uniflora

LILY FAMILY

This beautiful perennial lily grows from slender rhizomes, with the flowers appearing on short, leafless stalks. The flowers are about 5 cm in diameter, and are usually solitary, white, and cup-shaped, appearing at the top of an erect, hairy stalk. The plant has 2 or 3 leaves which are oblong or elliptical, shiny with hairy edges, and appear at the base of the flowering stalk.

The genus name, *Clintonia*, honours DeWitt Clinton, a New York state governor and botanist of the 19th century. As the season progresses, the flower is replaced by a single deep blue bead-like berry, giving the plant another common name of Beadlily. The bead was used by some Native peoples to make a blue dye.

Star Flowered Solomon's-Seal
Smilacina stellata

LILY FAMILY

A lily of moist woods, rivers and stream banks, thickets, and meadows, from montane to subalpine elevations. The flowers are white, star-shaped, and arrayed in a loose, short-stalked cluster, often on a zig-zag stem. The leaves are broadly lance-shaped, numerous and alternate, gradually tapering to a pointed tip, with prominent parallel veining, sometimes folded at the midline. The fruit is a cluster of green- to cream-coloured berries, with maroon to brown stripes.

One theory holds that the common name is a reference to the six-pointed star in the seal of King Solomon. The species name, *stellata*, is Greek for "star-like." There is another closely related species found in the same habitat—False Solomon's-Seal (*S. racemosa*), shown on page 75. The flowers of False Solomon's-Seal are much more numerous, and decidedly smaller than those of Star Flowered Solomon's-Seal. The flowers of False Solomon's-Seal were described by one observer as a "creamy foam of flowers," a rather apt description.

Sticky False Asphodel
Tofieldia glutinosa

LILY FAMILY

A lily of wet bogs, meadows, and stream banks, the distinctive feature of this plant is the upper portion of the flowering stem, which is glandular and sticky. The white flowers are clustered atop the stem, with dark anthers conspicuous against the white of the petals. The basal leaves are linear, lance-shaped, and grass-like, and are about half the length of the stem.

The plant resembles the European Asphodel, thus the common name. The genus name, *Tofieldia*, is to honour 18th-century British botanist Thomas Tofield. The species name, *glutinosa*, is a reference to the sticky stem below the flower. Mosquitoes are often trapped on the sticky stem of this plant, which acts as natural flypaper.

Three Spot Mariposa Lily
Calochortus apiculatus

LILY FAMILY

A plant of open coniferous woods, dry, sandy, or gravelly slopes, and moist fescue grassland from the montane to the subalpine zone. This perennial lily grows from a bulb as a single-leafed plant, producing 1–5 flowers from each plant. The flower is white to yellowish-white, with 3 spreading petals, fringed at the margins. Each petal is hairy on the inner surfaces, with a purplish gland at the base. These purple glands give the flower one of its common names— Three-Spot Tulip. Three narrow white sepals appear between the petals.

Mariposa means "butterfly" in Spanish, it being thought that the markings on some Mariposa lilies resemble the markings on a butterfly's wings. The genus name, *Calochortus*, is derived from the Greek *kallos*, meaning "beautiful," and *chortos*, meaning "grass." The species name, *apiculatus*, refers to the slender tipped anthers. Some Native tribes used the bulbs of the plant as food, it being eaten raw, cooked, or dried for later use. The Blackfoot looked upon them as famine food only. Picking the flower will destroy the plant because the bulb depends upon the flower for nutrients. Picking the flowers can significantly reduce the range and distribution of lilies. The plants do not transplant well, and cultivation attempts have consistently failed.

Western White Trillium (Western Wake Robin)
Trillium ovatum

LILY FAMILY

This gorgeous lily is rare in the area and prefers boggy, rich soils in the montane and lower subalpine forests. The distinctive leaves are large (up to 15 cm long), stalkless, broadly egg-shaped with a sharp tip, and occur in a whorl of 3 below the flower. The solitary white flower blooms atop a short stem above the leaves. The flower has 3 broad white petals up to 5 cm long, alternating with 3 narrow green sepals. The petals change colour with age, first turning pink, and then progressing to purple.

The common and genus names are derived from the Latin *trillium*, meaning "in threes," a reference to the leaves, petals, and sepals occurring in threes. The species name, *ovatum*, refers to the shape of the leaves. The plant is an early bloomer, which gives rise to its other common name, Wake Robin, it being said that the blooms and the robins arrive about the same time in the spring. Seeds from the plant are oil rich and attract ants. Ants carry the seeds to their nests, and thus distribute the seeds for the plant. Some Native peoples referred to the plant as "Birth Root," a reference to using the plant to reduce uterine bleeding during childbirth. The plant was first described for science by Frederick Pursh from a specimen collected in 1806 by Meriwether Lewis "on the rapids of the Columbia River." Trillium is the floral emblem of the Province of Ontario.

White Camas
Zigadenus elegans

LILY FAMILY

This plant of moist grasslands, grassy slopes, and open woods grows from an onion-like bulb that has no oniony smell. The greenish-white, foul-smelling flowers appear in open clusters along an erect stem. There are yellowish-green V-shaped glands (nectaries) near the base of the petals and sepals. The leaves are mainly basal and resemble grass, with prominent midveins.

The origin of the genus name, *Zigadenus* , is explained in the narrative on Death Camas (*Z. venenosus*), shown on page 73. The species name, *elegans*, means "elegant." Though elegant, indeed, these plants are extremely poisonous, containing very toxic alkaloids, particularly in the bulbs. These plants have been responsible for killing many people and animals. When the flowers are missing, White Camas and Death Camas are difficult to distinguish from Blue Camas, (*Camassia quamash*), shown on page 24, another lily, the bulb of which was commonly used as a food source by Native peoples and early settlers. Other common names for White Camas include Mountain Death Camas, Green Lily, and Showy Death Camas.

Northern Bedstraw
Galium boreale

MADDER FAMILY

A plant common to roadsides and woodlands in the montane to subalpine zones. The flowers are tiny, fragrant, and white, occurring in dense clusters at the top of the stems. The individual flowers are cruciform (cross-shaped), with each having 4 spreading petals that are joined at the base. There are no sepals. The smooth stems are square in cross-section, and bear whorls of 4 narrow, lance-shaped leaves, each with 3 veins.

The common name for this plant is a reference to a practice of Native peoples to use the dried, sweet-smelling plants to stuff mattresses. The roots of the plants were a source of red and yellow dyes. The genus name, *Galium*, is derived from the Greek *gala*, which means "milk," a reference to the fact that country folk used to use the juice of another similar plant to curdle milk. The species name, *boreale*, means "northern," a reference to the circumpolar distribution of the plant.

Sweet-Scented Bedstraw
Galium triflorum

MADDER FAMILY

This plant occurs in moist mountain forests, along stream banks, and in dense, damp woods. It is a low, trailing perennial that has leaves in whorls of 6, radiating from a common centre stem. The leaves are tipped with a sharp point. The leaves give off a sweet aroma, variously compared to vanilla or cinnamon. The flowers are small, greenish-white, and occur in groups of 3 in the leaf axils, with 4 petals per flower.

The common name, Bedstraw, is derived from the practice of some Native peoples of using the plant for stuffing their mattresses. Another member of the genus, Northern Bedstraw (*G. boreale*), shown on page 83, occurs in similar habitat, and was used in the same fashion.

Silver Rock Cress (Alpine Smelowskia)
Smelowskia calycina
MUSTARD FAMILY

This plant is a matting perennial that inhabits rocky ledges, scree slopes, ridges, and rocky crests in the subalpine and alpine zones. The whole plant is covered with soft, dense, felt-like, grey hair. The basal leaves are blue-grey, and may be lance-shaped or deeply cleft into several lobes. The stem leaves are smaller and finely dissected, like fern leaves. The several stems can reach 20 cm tall. The creamy white, or sometimes pink to pale purple, four-petaled flowers bloom in clusters at the top of the stems.

The genus name, *Smelowskia*, honours 19th-century Russian botanist Timotheus Smelowsky. Fern-Leaved Candytuft is another common name for the plant. This species is often infected by an invasive rust fungus that extracts nutrients from the plant, and, in the process, causes the flowers to abort and the leaves to disfigure. See photograph on the right above.

Blunt-Leaved Bog Orchid
Habenaria obtusata (also *Platanthera obtusata*)

ORCHID FAMILY

The solitary leaf and small, greenish-white flowers of this bog orchid make it easy to distinguish from other local orchids. The single basal leaf is oblong and blunt on the end, tapering to the sheathing base. The stem grows up to about 20 cm tall, with the flowers distributed up the stem. The flowers have a strap-shaped lip, and a tapering spur which is about as long as the lip.

The genus name, *Habenaria*, is derived from the Latin *habena*, meaning "rein," a reference to the rein-like appendages on the lip. The species name, *obtusata*, means "blunt," a reference to the shape of the single leaf. The species is pollinated by mosquitoes, which are usually in no short supply in the habitat of this lovely orchid.

Bracted Orchid
Habenaria viridis

ORCHID FAMILY

This handsome orchid grows in open woods, moist meadows, and damp grassy slopes almost to timberline. It is an erect plant that reaches heights of 40 cm, and has long, tapering bracts that stand out from the flowering stalk. Among the bracts, almost hidden by them, lie the small, green flowers. Each flower has a spur and a small, distinctive lip. The lip is spoon or spatula-shaped, and may be streaked with purple. The lip broadens at the tip, ending in 2 or 3 pronounced teeth. The spur is about half as long as the lip. Several dark green, lance-shaped leaves ascend the stem, growing smaller as they approach the flowering spike.

The genus name, *Habenaria*, is derived from the Latin *habena*, meaning "reins," a reference to the rein-like appendage on the lip of some members of the genus. The species name, *viridis*, refers to the green colour of the flowers.

Heart-Leaved Twayblade
Listera cordata

ORCHID FAMILY

This small orchid, standing about 15 cm high, prefers a cool, damp, mossy habitat. As a consequence of its size and preferred location, it is an easy flower to miss. The white flowers are scattered up the stem in an open raceme. The lip of the flower in this species is deeply split, almost in two. The stem leaf structure of the genus is distinctive, with 2 leaves appearing opposite each other partway up the stem.

The common name, Twayblade, refers to the 2 leaves that appear on opposite sides of the stem, about halfway up the stem. The genus name, *Listera*, commemorates Dr. Martin Lister, an English naturalist of the 1600s. The species name, *cordata*, means "heart-shaped," a reference to the shape of the stem leaves.

Hooded Ladies' Tresses
Spiranthes romanzoffiana

ORCHID FAMILY

This orchid is reasonably common in the Rocky Mountains and can stand up to 60 cm high. The characteristic feature of the plant is the crowded flower spike, which can contain up to 60 densely spaced white flowers that appear to coil around the end of the stem in 3 spiraling ranks. When newly bloomed, the flower has a wonderful aroma, which most people say smells like vanilla.

The common name of the plant is a reference to the braid-like appearance of the flowers, similar to a braid in a lady's hair. The genus name is derived from the Greek *speira*, meaning "coil," and *anthos*, meaning "flower," referring to the spiral inflorescence. The species name honours Russian Count Nicholas Romanzoff, a 19th-century Russian minister of state and patron of science. The species was first discovered on the Aleutian island of Unalaska, when Alaska was still a Russian territory.

Mountain Lady's Slipper
Cypripedium montanum

ORCHID FAMILY

This distinctive and rare orchid grows up to 60 cm tall, and occurs in dry to moist woods and open areas from mid to subalpine elevations in the Rocky Mountains. The lower petal forms a white, pouch-shaped lower lip that has purple markings. The sepals and lateral petals are brownish, have wavy margins, and appear to spiral away from the stem. The leaves are alternate, broadly elliptical, clasping on the stem, and have prominent veins. One to three flowers appear on the stem, and they are wonderfully fragrant.

The genus name, *Cypripedium*, is derived from the Greek *kupris*, meaning "Aphrodite," the Greek goddess of love and beauty, and *pedilon*, meaning "foot" or "slipper," thus Aphrodite's slipper. The species name, *montanum*, means "of the mountains." This plant is relatively rare in its natural habitat, and has been made more so by indiscriminate picking and attempts at transplantation—which virtually never are successful. The plant depends upon the flower for nutrition, and picking the flower will kill the plant. Several other Lady's Slippers occur in the area, the Yellow Lady's Slipper (*C. calceolus*) being the most common.

Rattlesnake Plantain
Goodyera oblongifolia
ORCHID FAMILY

This orchid grows in shaded, dry or moist coniferous woods in the Rocky Mountains. It is a single-stemmed, stiff-hairy perennial that grows up to 40 cm tall. The basal leaves are distinctive, with a white, mottled midvein, and whitish lateral veins. The robust downy spike bears small greenish-white flowers in a loose one-sided or twisted raceme, with the lower flowers blooming first. The lip of the flower has a wide open mouth, pressed up against the overhanging hood.

The common name originates from the mottled white markings on the leaves, which reminded early European settlers of the markings on a rattlesnake. Plantain comes from the Latin *planta*, meaning "foot," a reference to the broad, flat, foot-like leaves. The genus name commemorates the 17th-century English botanist John Goodyer.

Sparrow's-Egg Lady's Slipper (Franklin's Lady's Slipper)
Cypripedium passerinum

ORCHID FAMILY

This lovely orchid grows from a cord-like rhizome in boggy areas, along streams, and in mossy coniferous areas in the lower subalpine zone. It resembles both Yellow Lady's Slipper (*C. calceolus*) and Mountain Lady's Slipper (*C. montanum*) in shape, but this flower is smaller, has bright purple dots on the interior, and has shorter, stubbier, greenish sepals. Both the stem and the leaves of the plant are covered in soft hairs.

The origin of the genus name is explained in the note on Mountain Lady's Slipper, shown on page 90. The species name, *passerinum*, means "sparrow-like," a reference to the spotting on the flower being like the markings on a sparrow egg. Care should be taken when moving around these orchids. They are fragile and easily damaged. Picking the flower is anathema—the flower will quickly wilt, and the plant will die without the nutrition provided by the flower.

Tall White Bog Orchid
Habenaria dilatata (also *Platanthera dilatata*)

ORCHID FAMILY

As the common name suggests, this plant favours wet ground, shaded woods, bogs, pond edges, and streamside environments. It grows up to a metre tall, and produces white to greenish, sweet-scented flowers in a spike-like cluster, with flowers distributed along the stalk. The flowers are waxy and small, with the lowest petal forming a lip that widens at the base. The flower also has a slender, curved spur. The lance-shaped leaves are prominently veined and fleshy, short at the base, longest in the middle of the plant, and shorter at the top.

The genus name, *Habenaria*, is derived from the Latin *habena*, meaning "rein," a reference to the rein-like appendages on the lip. The species name, *dilatata*, means "dilated," a reference to the expanded base of the lip on the flower. When blooming, this flower has a heavenly scent, variously described as of vanilla, mock orange, and cloves. Some Native peoples believed the plant to be poisonous to humans and animals, and used an extract from the plant to sprinkle on baits for coyotes and grizzlies.

Mountain Chickweed (Alpine Chickweed)
Cerastium beeringianum

PINK FAMILY

This plant inhabits exposed alpine ridges, where it often forms matted clumps. The stems are up to 25 cm tall, and are hairy and sticky to the touch. The leaves are lance to spatula-shaped, covered with silky hairs, and attached directly to the base, without a stalk. The flowers are white, and have 5 petals, each with a prominent cleft at the tip. The sepals have translucent margins, and are pencilled with purple.

This species is also sometimes referred to as Bering Chickweed. Mountain Chickweed is similar to Mouse-Eared Chickweed (*C. arvense*), which appears at lower elevations. Another Chickweed that appears in a similar environment is the Long-Stalked Chickweed (*Stellaria monantha*). It too has 5 white petals, but the clefts in its petals are so deep that the flower appears to have 10 petals. The name Chickweed originated with the practice of feeding species of the genus to chickens, goslings, and caged birds.

Sweet-Flowered Androsace (Rock Jasmine)
Androsace chamaejasme

PRIMROSE FAMILY

This striking low-growing cushion plant is seldom more than 10 cm tall, but can form mats of flowers on rocky ledges and fields. The flowers are borne on a single, white-hairy stem, and they occur in umbels of 4 or 5 flowers. The petals of the flowers are white, with a yellow or orange eye. Though small, the wonderful aroma of these flowers is worth getting down on hands and knees to smell.

The genus name, *Androsace*, is derived from the Greek *androsakes*, a marine plant. The species name, *chamaejasme*, is from the Greek *chamae*, meaning "dwarf" or "low on the ground," and *jasme*, meaning "jasmine," thus a common name for the plant—Rock Jasmine.

Alpine Spring Beauty
Claytonia megarhiza

PURSLANE FAMILY

This beautiful plant grows from a fleshy, swollen taproot on alpine scree slopes. It strongly resembles Western Spring Beauty (*C. lanceolata*), but this plant has spoon-shaped, reddish-green basal leaves and reddish tinged stems, and it grows from a taproot. Western Spring Beauty arises from a small corm.

The origin of the genus name is discussed under Western Spring Beauty, shown on page 97. The species name, *megarhiza*, refers to the taproot from which the plant grows. The plant is sometimes referred to as Tufted Spring Beauty.

Western Spring Beauty
Claytonia lanceolata

URSLANE FAMILY

The flowers of this early-blooming plant are white, but may appear pink, owing to the reddish veins in the petals, and the pink anthers. The tips of the petals are distinctly notched. The plants are usually less than 20 cm tall, and the flowers appear in loose, terminal short-stalked clusters. The plant grows from a small, white, edible corm.

The genus name, *Claytonia*, honours John Clayton, a 17th-century botanist who collected plants in what was to become the United States. The species name, *lanceolata*, refers to the lance-shaped leaves. The Western Spring Beauty is in the same family as the Bitterroot (*Lewisia rediviva*), and like the Bitterroot, was used by Native peoples as food. Bears and rodents also make use of the corms of the plant for food. Ungulates often eat the flowers and leaves. Alpine Spring Beauty (*C. megarhiza*), shown on page 96, is a relatively rare, but similar plant that occurs in the alpine zone. It has spoon-shaped, reddish-green, basal leaves, and grows from a fleshy, swollen taproot.

Birch-Leaf Spirea
Spiraea betulifolia

ROSE FAMILY

This deciduous shrub grows to heights of 70 cm, and occurs in moist to dry, open and wooded sites from valley floors to the subalpine zone. It spreads by underground runners, and often forms dense cover on the forest floor. The plant is alternately branched, with cinnamon-brown bark, and alternate oval or egg-shaped leaves that are irregularly coarse-toothed towards the tip. The flowers are dull white, often tinged to purple or pink, saucer-shaped, and occur in flat-topped clusters on the ends of the stems.

The genus name, *Spiraea*, is derived from the Greek *speira*, meaning "spire" or "wreath," possibly a reference to the plant being used as a garland. The species name, *betulifolia*, means "leaves like a birch," the reference being to the similarity of Spirea leaves to those of birch trees. A common name for the plant is White Meadowsweet. Native peoples and herbalists have long used the plant to relieve pain, reduce inflammations, and treat a variety of other ailments from heartburn to abdominal and menstrual pains. The branches of the plant were also used for drying and smoking fish. A similar species, Mountain Spirea, also known as Pink Meadowsweet (*S. densiflora*) occurs in the same area, but it has rose to pink flat-topped clusters of flowers.

Partridgefoot (Creeping Spiraea)
Luetkea pectinata
ROSE FAMILY

Lorna Allen image

This dwarf evergreen shrub creates extensive mats, as it creeps over the ground in moist meadows, scree slopes, and shady areas near timberline. It often grows where snow melts late in the season. The leaves are mainly basal, numerous, smooth, fan-shaped, and much divided. Old leaves wither and persist for long periods of time. The white to cream-coloured flowers appear in short, crowded clusters atop erect stems. The flowers have 4 to 6 pistils, and about 20 stamens, which are conspicuous on the flowers.

The genus name, *Luetkea*, honours Count F. P. Lutke, a 19th-century Russian sea captain and explorer. This is the only species in the genus. The species name, *pectinata*, means "with narrow divisions—like the teeth of a comb," and is a reference to the leaf structure of the plant. The common name, Partridgefoot, is derived from the supposed resemblance between the leaves of the species and the footprint of a partridge. Given the alpine habitat of this plant, it might be more appropriately called Ptarmiganfoot.

Thimbleberry
Rubus parviflorus
ROSE FAMILY

A plant that often forms thickets on avalanche slopes, and the margins of forests and streams. The plant is closely related to the Raspberry, but this vigorous shrub does not have prickles or spines. The plant can grow up to 2 m tall. It has large leaves, each with 3–5 lobes, with jagged-toothed margins, resembling a maple leaf in shape. The flowers are white, with a central core of yellow stamens. There are usually 3–5 flowers in clusters at the ends of branches. The bright red fruit looks like a flattened raspberry, but it is rather tasteless and very seedy.

Native peoples peeled the young shoots of Thimbleberry and ate it raw, or cooked it with meat in stews. The large leaves were widely used as temporary containers, to line baskets, and to separate items in the same basket. They also make a good biodegradable toilet tissue substitute when needed.

Trailing Raspberry
Rubus pubescens
ROSE FAMILY

This dwarf shrub is a low, trailing plant with slender runners and erect flowering stems that grows at low to subalpine elevations in moist to wet forests and clearings. The plant has soft hairs on it, but no prickles like Wild Red Raspberry (*R. idaeus*). The leaves are palmately divided into 3 oval or diamond-shaped leaflets, with pointed tips, and toothed margins. The flowers are white and spreading, and occur on short erect branches. The fruits are red drupelets—the aggregate cluster makes up a raspberry.

Native peoples used this plant as a food source and for medicinal purposes, similarly to Wild Red Raspberry, shown on page 104. Trailing Raspberry is sometimes referred to as Dewberry.

Western Mountain Ash

Sorbus scopulina

ROSE FAMILY

This deciduous, erect to spreading shrub grows to heights of 4 m in moist open or shaded places from the foothills to the subalpine zones. The branches are slightly white-hairy and sticky when new; reddish-grey to yellowish when mature. The leaves are alternate and pinnately compound—leaflets appearing opposite each other on both sides of a common axis—with 11–13 leaflets per leaf. The leaflets are sharply tipped and sharply toothed from tip to base. The flowers are white and saucer-shaped, with 5 broad petals, and they occur in large flat-topped clusters. The fruits are glossy orange to red berry-like pomes in dense clusters.

Some Native peoples ate the pomes of this plant, but most looked upon them as inedible. Some tribes boiled the peeled branches or inner bark of the plant to make medicinal concoctions. The plant is used quite extensively as a garden ornamental. The fruit clusters are a favoured food of a variety of bird species.

White Dryad (White Mountain Avens)
Dryas octopetala
ROSE FAMILY

This dwarf evergreen grows close to the ground, forming mats on gravelly soil in the alpine zone. The leaves are oblong to lance-shaped, leathery, dark green, with edges that are scalloped and often rolled under. The creamy-coloured flowers bloom in abundance soon after snows melt. The flowers are borne on short, hairy, leafless stems that rise from the mats of leaves. Each flower has 8 petals, thus the species name *octopetala*. The fruits are similar to those of the Yellow Mountain Avens (*D. drummondii*), shown on page 150.

The genus is named after Dryas, the wood nymph in Greek mythology. This plant is superbly adapted to its harsh natural environment. The plant has root nodules that store nitrogen in a nutrient-poor habitat. White Dryad is also valued by rock-gardeners as a ground cover.

Wild Red Raspberry
Rubus idaeus

ROSE FAMILY

This erect to spreading deciduous shrub grows up to 2 m tall at low to subalpine elevations in clearings, along streams, and in disturbed areas. It is similar to cultivated raspberry in appearance. The prickly branches (or canes) are biennial, and are green in the first year, and yellowish brown to cinnamon brown in the second. The leaves are palmately divided (i.e. divided into leaflets that diverge from a common point) into 3–5 egg-shaped, pointed, double saw-toothed leaflets. The flowers are white and drooping, occurring singly or in small clusters. The fruits are juicy red drupelets—a drupelet being one part of an aggregate fruit—in dense clusters, the totality of which is the raspberry. Other examples of fruits that appear as drupelets include blackberries and thimbleberries.

Native peoples made extensive use of Wild Red Raspberries as a food source and for medicinal purposes. A tea brewed from the plant was administered to women to ease the pain of childbirth, and the concoction was also used to treat a variety of other conditions, such as boils, bladder infections, liver problems, and diarrhea. Modern herbalists also value this plant for a variety of conditions. Pharmacologists have validated raspberry leaf as an antispasmodic.

Wild Strawberry
Fragaria virginiana

ROSE FAMILY

A plant of shaded to open gravelly soils and thickets, from prairie to alpine habitats. The single, five-petaled, white flower appears on a leafless stem that is usually shorter than the leaves are long. The stamens are numerous and yellow. The leaves are rounded to broadly oval, toothed, with 3 leaflets on short stalks. The fruit is a red berry, covered with sunken, seed-like achenes. New plants are often established from reddish runners.

"Strawberry" is said to come from the Anglo-Saxon name *streowberie* because the runners from the plant are strewn across the ground. The genus name, *Fragaria*, means "fragrance." Strawberry plants are rich in iron, calcium, potassium, sodium, and vitamin C. The fruits are delicious, with a more pronounced flavour than domestic strawberries. The leaves have been used to make tea, and have also been used for medicinal purposes.

Pale Comandra (Bastard Toadflax)
Comandra umbellata

SANDALWOOD FAMILY

This erect, blue-green perennial is common in open pine woods, gravel slopes and grasslands, and springs from a creeping rootstalk. The leaves are lance-shaped and hug the erect stem. The flowers occur in a rounded or flat-topped cluster atop the stem. Each flower is greenish-white, with the sepals separated above and fused into a small funnel below.

The genus name, *Comandra*, is derived from the Greek *kome*, meaning "hair," and *andros*, meaning "man," probably a reference to the hairy bases of the stamens on the flower. The species name, *umbellata*, is a reference to the shape of the cluster of flowers. The plant has another common name—Bastard Toadflax—though the plant bears no relationship to toadflax, and is not in any way similar. Pale Comandra is a parasite, taking water, and perhaps food, from its host plant.

Alaska Saxifrage
Saxifraga ferruginea

SAXIFRAGE FAMILY

This plant grows in moist soils, on rocky outcrops, and along spring banks in the subalpine and alpine zones. The leaves are basal only, hairy, and wedge-shaped with toothed margins. The numerous white flowers bloom in an open inflorescence on hairy stems. The flowers have 5 petals. The 3 upper petals are broader than the lower 2 petals, have yellow spots, and abruptly narrow at the base. Some of the flowers on the plant may become leafy bulblets and drop off the plant.

The origin of the genus name, *Saxifraga*, is explained in the note on Purple Saxifrage (*S. oppositifolia*), shown on page 32. The species name, *ferruginea*, is derived from the Latin *ferrum*, which means "iron," a reference to the rusty colour of the calyx. That rusty colour gives rise to another common name, Rusty Saxifrage.

Bishop's-Cap (Mitrewort)
Mitella nuda

SAXIFRAGE FAMILY

This wonderful plant occurs in moist to dry forests, bogs, thickets, and along streams, from the aspen parklands to the subalpine elevations. The plant stands erect and grows up to 20 cm tall. The leaves are basal, heart- to kidney-shaped, and short-lobed, with rounded teeth. The flowers are tiny and occur in an open cluster, scattered up the leafless stem. The saucer-shaped flowers are very distinctive, and when examined closely remind one of some kind of a satellite dish, complete with antennae festooned around the circumference of the flower.

The genus name, *Mitella*, is derived from the Greek *mitra*, which means "a cap," a reference to the flower's resemblance to a mitre—the hat worn by bishops—ergo, Bishop's Cap. The species name, *nuda*, means "naked," most probably a reference to the leafless stem of the plant. This plant is one of the most fascinating in the forest.

Foamflower
Tiarella trifoliata
SAXIFRAGE FAMILY

These beautiful flowers inhabit moist coniferous woods, stream banks, and trails from the boreal forest to the subalpine zone. The plant grows up to 50 cm in height, and the flowers are white or pinkish, arranged in open panicles well above the leaves. The leaves are compound, usually with 3 leaflets. The middle leaflet is usually three-lobed and toothed.

The genus name, *Tiarella*, is derived from the Latin *tiara*, an ancient Persian turban-like headdress. The species name, *trifoliata*, refers to the compound leaf with 3 leaflets. Other common names applied to the plant are Laceflower and False Mitrewort.

Green Saxifrage (Northern Golden Saxifrage)
Chrysosplenium tetrandrum

SAXIFRAGE FAMILY

Cliff Wallis image

This perennial has weak, somewhat erect stems, that grow up to 20 cm high in rock crevices, along streams, in seepage areas, and in shady sites from the montane to the alpine zones. The leaves are alternate and mainly basal, on slender stalks up to 3 cm long, oval to kidney-shaped, and have 3–7 broad scallops. The flowers are inconspicuous and small, greenish with purple dots, with a four-lobed calyx, and attached to the lower half of the ovary.

The genus name, *Chrysosplenium*, is derived from the Greek *chrysos*, which means "golden," and *splen*, which means "spleen," a reference to a supposed medicinal quality of the plant. The species name, *tetrandrum*, refers to the flower parts which occur in fours. The plant is also known by the common name Northern Water Carpet, which accurately describes the matted form assumed by the plant in wet habitats it favours.

Leather-Leaved Saxifrage
Leptarrhena pyrolifolia

SAXIFRAGE FAMILY

This plant occurs in wet, open forests, wet meadows, along streams, and in seeps in the subalpine and alpine zones. The leaves are mostly basal, oval to oblong, leathery, prominently veined, and have toothed edges. The purplish stems are erect to heights of up to 40 cm, and have only 1–3 small leaves. The flowers are small and white, sometimes pink, and appear in tight clusters at the top of the flowering stem. Each flower has 10 long stamens. The fruits are paired, pointed, purplish-red, single-chambered capsules in clusters atop the stem.

The genus name, *Leptarrhena*, is derived from the Greek *lepto*, which means "slender," and *arrhen*, which means "male," a reference to the slender stamens on the plant. The species name, *pyrolifolia*, most probably is a reference to the leaves, *Pyrola* being the genus of many Wintergreens, which have leathery leaves. This plant has been enthusiastically adopted by rock gardeners.

Red-Stemmed Saxifrage
Saxifraga lyallii

SAXIFRAGE FAMILY

This plant occurs on stream banks, seepage areas, and other wet places in the high subalpine and alpine zones, and is often found growing in wet mosses at such elevations. The leaves are basal, fan- to wedge-shaped, coarsely toothed, and abruptly narrowing on long stalks. The flowering stems grow to heights of 30 cm, and each bears 1 to several tiny, white, star-shaped flowers on its upper parts. When mature, the white petals are marked with greenish-yellow blotches, and the sepals are reflexed. The fruits are two- to four-pointed, bright red capsules.

The plant is also known as Lyall's Saxifrage, named in honour of David Lyall, a 19th-century Scottish botanist who collected a number of North American plants. As a group, Saxifrages have some of the most intricate and interesting flower conformations in the area, and all are worth examining closely.

Round-Leaved Alumroot
Heuchera cylindrica

SAXIFRAGE FAMILY

This robust perennial can grow to heights approaching a metre, and can be widespread and common on dry plateaus, open forests, and rocky outcrops. The leaves are all basal, and are heart- or kidney-shaped. The cream to greenish-yellow flowers are somewhat bell-shaped, and grouped at the top of a tall, thin, leafless stem. The flowers have a decidedly hairy appearance.

Alumroot was important for medicinal purposes for Native peoples. It works as a styptic for stopping bleeding and closing wounds. These plants are still used by herbalists. The root of the plant is a very intense astringent (like alum), thus the common name for the plant. The genus name, *Heuchera*, is to honour Johann Heinrich von Heucher, an 18th-century German botanist and physician. Alumroot is also used as a mordant to fix dyes, and many people prefer it to the manufactured alternatives. This plant is sometimes called Sticky Alumroot, a reference to the sticky, glandular hairs on the upper stem.

Spotted Saxifrage
Saxifraga bronchialis

SAXIFRAGE FAMILY

These beautiful flowers inhabit rocky crevices, rock faces, screes, and open slopes, often appearing as if by magic from the rocks. The white flowers appear in clusters at the top of the wiry brown stems, and have small red or yellow spots near the tips of the 5 petals. A close examination of this beautiful flower is well worth the time.

The origin of the genus name, *Saxifraga*, is explained in the note on Purple Saxifrage (*S. oppositifolia*), shown on page 32. The species name, *bronchialis*, is from the Latin *bronchus*, meaning "branch" or "division," a reference to the branching, mat-like growth of the plant.

Sitka Valerian
Valeriana sitchensis

VALERIAN FAMILY

This perennial grows up to 80 cm tall and has a somewhat succulent, squarish stem. It occurs in moist subalpine and alpine environments, in alpine meadows, and along streams. The leaves are large and opposite, divided into 3–7 coarsely toothed lobes, with progressively shorter petioles up the stem. The numerous tubular flowers are crowded into a nearly flat-topped cluster at the top of the stem. The buds and young flowers are a pale lavender colour, but the flowers later fade to white. The floral tubes are notched into 5 equal lobes

There appear to be two schools of thought as to where this genus gets its name. One school opines that the genus name is from Valeria, a Roman province in southern Europe, now a part of Hungary. The other school contends that the genus name comes from the Latin *valere*, meaning "to be healthy," a reference to the fact that the plant has long been used for various medicinal purposes. The species name, *sitchensis*, is from Sitka Sound in southeastern Alaska, where the species was first collected and described. Two common names for the plant are Wild Heliotrope and Tobacco Root. The Tobacco Root Range in Montana takes its name from the plant. Valerian is the original source of diazepam, a tranquilizer and muscle relaxant commonly known as Valium.

Mist Maiden (Cliff Romanzoffia)
Romanzoffia sitchensis

WATERLEAF FAMILY

Lorna Allen image

This dainty, smooth, tufted perennial is fairly rare in the Canadian Rocky Mountains, and occurs on moist rocky cliffs and ledges, only in the subalpine and alpine zones. The leaves are mostly basal, kidney-shaped, and have 5–9 lobes. The white to cream-coloured flowers are borne in loose clusters on thin stems above the leaves. The flowers are five-petaled and funnel-shaped at the base, each with a yellow eye.

The genus name, *Romanzoffia*, honours Count Nikolai Romanzoff, a 19th-century Russian patron of science who sponsored scientific explorations. The plant was first discovered in Sitka Sound in Alaska, whence comes the species name.

Silverleaf Phacelia (Scorpionweed)
Phacelia hastata
WATERLEAF FAMILY

This tap-rooted perennial grows up to 50 cm tall, and occurs from low to subalpine elevations in dry basins, gravelly areas, and roadsides. The leaves are elliptic with prominent veins, and generally are covered with silvery hairs. The flowers are white to lavender, funnel-shaped, and occur in compact clusters that spiral up the stem. The flowers have 5 broad petal lobes, 5 narrow hairy sepals, and 5 long stamens that extend well past the petals.

The common name, Scorpionweed, most probably arises because some people say the coiled branches of the flower clusters resemble the tail of a scorpion. The species is called Silverleaf because of the fine, silvery hairs on the leaves. The genus name, *Phacelia*, is derived from the Greek *phakelos*, meaning "bundle" or "cluster," a reference to the appearance of the flowers. The species name, *hastata*, is derived from the Latin *hastatus*, meaning "spear," a reference to the spearhead shape of some of the leaves.

Yellow Flowers

This section includes flowers that are predominantly yellow when encountered in the field. The colour varies from bright yellow to pale cream. Some of the flowers in this section have other colour variations and you might have to check other sections of the book to find the flower. For example, the Paintbrushes (*Castilleja* spp.) have a yellow variation, but they are most often encountered in a red colour and they have been pictured in that section for purposes of sorting.

Yellow Buckwheat (Umbrella Plant)
Eriogonum flavum
BUCKWHEAT FAMILY

This fuzzy-haired tufted perennial favours dry, often sandy or rocky outcrops, eroded slopes, and badlands. The leaves are dark green on top, but appear white to felty on the underside due to the dense hairs. The yellow flowers occur in compound umbels—umbrella shaped clusters—atop the stem. The common name for the plant, Umbrella Plant, is testimony to the shape of the inflorescence.

The genus name, *Eriogonum*, is derived from the Greek *erion*, meaning "wool," and *gonu*, meaning "knee or joint." *Flavum* means "yellow." The plant has an unpleasant smell, but the nectar is relished by bees, and produces a strongly flavoured buckwheat-like honey.

Alpine Buttercup
Ranunculus eschscholtzii

BUTTERCUP FAMILY

This Buttercup can reach heights of 30 cm, and lives near or above timber-line, appearing beside streams or ponds, near snowdrifts, and around late snowmelt. The leaves are mainly basal, sometimes deeply lobed, and round to kidney-shaped. The flowering stems are hairless and may accommodate up to 3 flowers. The flowers are bright yellow, with 5 petals and 5 purple-tinged sepals. Stamens and pistils are numerous.

The genus name, *Ranunculus*, is derived from the Greek *rana*, which means "frog," a reference to the wet habitat preferred by many members of the genus. The species name, *eschscholtzii*, honours Johann Friedrich Gustav von Eschscholtz, a 19th-century German surgeon and professor of anatomy who accompanied two Russian explorations of the Pacific coast of North America. The California Poppy (*Eschscholzia californica*) is also named for him. Alpine Buttercup is also known locally as Mountain Buttercup, Snow Buttercup, and Snowpack Buttercup.

Yellow Columbine
Aquilegia flavescens

BUTTERCUP FAMILY

Lemon yellow in colour, these beautiful flowers nod at the ends of slender stems that lift the flowers above the leaves. Each flower is composed of 5 wing-shaped sepals, and 5 tube-shaped petals that are flaring at the open end and tapering to a distinctive spur at the opposite end. The plant occurs in the alpine and subalpine zones.

The origin of the genus name, *Aquilegia*, is the subject of some debate. One school holds that it is from the Latin *aquila*, meaning "eagle," and is a reference to the long, talon-like spur on the flower. Another school argues that the genus name is from *aqua*, meaning "water," and *legere*, meaning "collect," a reference to the drops of nectar that collect at the end of the spur. The common name, Columbine, is derived from *columba*, meaning "dove," it being said that the petals resembled a group of doves. Bumblebees and butterflies favour the Columbines.

Heart-Leaved Alexanders
Zizia aptera

CARROT FAMILY

This is a plant that occurs from prairies to the alpine zone in moist meadows, open woods, stream banks, and wetland margins. The small bright yellow flowers are numerous and occur in compound, flat-topped clusters at the top of the stems. The lower leaves are leathery, dark green, and heart-shaped. The stem leaves are smaller and divided into 3 leaflets. The stem leaves become progressively smaller along the stem until they become cleft leaflets. The flowers appear on top of hollow stems that are erect, and reach heights of up to 60 cm.

The origin of the name Alexanders is unknown. The genus name, *Zizia*, honours an early German botanist, Johann Baptist Ziz. The species name, *aptera*, means "wingless," probably a reference to the shape of the fruit of the plant.

Alpine Goldenrod
Solidago multiradiata

COMPOSITE FAMILY

This erect plant grows from a woody rootstock on dry, open slopes in the subalpine and alpine zones. The leaves are alternate, and often have a reddish appearance. The basal leaves and lower stem leaves are broadly lance- or spoon-shaped, slightly toothed or entire, with hairy margins. The flowers are yellow, and occur in loose or dense, narrow, long clusters atop the stem. Each flower is composed of 8 ray florets, surrounding 13 or more disk florets. There are several blunt-ended, reddish, hairy-margined bracts below the flower heads.

The genus name, *Solidago*, is derived from the Latin *solidus*, meaning "whole," and *ago*, meaning "to do or to make," a reference to the supposed healing properties of plants of this genus. Goldenrods were often used medicinally to treat a variety of ailments, from headaches, to nausea, to stomach ailments. The species name, *multiradiata*, refers to the numerous ray florets in the flowers. Dwarf Goldenrod (*S. spathulata*) is a related species occurring in similar habitat, but it does not have hairs on the margins of the basal leaves.

Alpine Hawk's-Beard (Dwarf Hawk's-Beard)
Crepis nana

COMPOSITE FAMILY

Cleve Wershler image

This dwarf perennial grows as a cushion plant on rocky alpine slopes and screes, and is firmly attached to its harsh environment by a long taproot. The leaves are bluish-green, spoon-shaped with long stems, and form a flat rosette tight to the ground. The bright yellow flowers appear on short stalks, hardly taller than the leaves. Each plant might produce 6–12 flowers, each with yellow ray flowers and no disk flowers. The fruits are dark purplish-brown achenes, with a pappus of fine, white, hair-like bristles at the top

The genus name, *Crepis*, is derived from the Greek *krepis*, meaning "boot" or "sandal," and it may be a reference to the deeply cut leaves of some members of the genus, which may suggest the thongs of a sandal. The name Hawk's-Beard was given to the genus *Crepis* by the botanist Asa Gray, and it might refer to the pappus' resemblance to the bristly feathers that surround a hawk's beak. It is said that the flower heads bloom close to the rosette of leaves in order to keep the developing ovaries in the warmest stratum of air, close to the ground and sun-warmed rocks.

Arrow-Leaved Groundsel (Giant Ragwort)
Senecio triangularis

COMPOSITE FAMILY

This leafy, lush perennial herb often grows to heights of one and a half metres, and occurs in large clumps in moist to wet, open or partly shaded sites, from the foothills to alpine elevations. The leaves are alternate, spearhead- or arrowhead-shaped, squared off at the base, and tapered to the point. The leaves are numerous and well developed along the whole stem of the plant. They are widest near the middle of the stem, and are coarsely sharp-toothed. The flowers occur in flat-topped clusters at the top of the plant, and have 5–8 bright yellow ray florets surrounding a disk of bright yellow to orange florets.

The genus name, *Senecio*, is derived from the Latin *senex*, which means "old man." Two opinions emerge as to the intended reference to old man. One says that it is because the receptacle to which the flowers are attached is free of hairs, ergo, hairless or bald, like an old man. The other says that the reference is to the grey or white hairs of many members of the genus, ergo, white-haired, like an old man. The species name, *triangularis*, refers to the shape of the leaves, a distinguishing feature of the plant. The common name, Ragwort, is said to be a reference to the ragged appearance of the leaf margins in many members of the genus. Many members of the genus contain poisonous alkaloids, but livestock seem to find the plants unpalatable.

Black-Tipped Groundsel
Senecio lugens

COMPOSITE FAMILY

This is a perennial that occurs on moist subalpine slopes and in alpine meadows. The leaves are mostly clustered at the base, erect, and surround the stem. There may be a few small, narrow stem leaves. The flowers are typical of the Groundsels—bright yellow lance-shaped ray florets surrounding yellow to orange disk florets. In this species, the bracts below the flowers have conspicuous black tips, a useful feature in the identification of the species; the bracts on other Groundsels being green.

The plant was first collected and described by Sir John Richardson, an Arctic explorer and naturalist who accompanied Sir John Franklin on two of his Arctic expeditions. The plant was collected near a place called Bloody Fall on the Coppermine River, in what is now Nunavut. Bloody Fall was the site of a massacre of a number of Inuit in 1771, and the Inuit that Richardson met near the site were fearful and respectful of the site, even years after the massacre. In sympathy with the Natives, Richardson named the species *lugens*, which is derived from the Latin word *lugere*, which means "to mourn."

Dwarf Mountain Groundsel
Senecio fremontii

COMPOSITE FAMILY

This dwarf species of Groundsel grows in rounded, matting clusters on gravel and rocks, and on scree slopes in the subalpine and alpine zones. The leaves are alternate, succulent, lance- to wedge-shaped, bright to light green, and coarsely toothed to incised on the margins. The bright yellow flowers, typical of Groundsels, cover the masses of leaves.

The origin of the genus name, *Senecio*, is explained in the narrative on Arrow-Leaved Groundsel (*S. triangularis*), shown on page 125. The plant was first collected in 1842 by John Charles Fremont, a 19th-century American soldier and explorer, in the Wind River Range in what is now the state of Montana. The species name, *fremontii*, honours Fremont.

Golden Fleabane
Erigeron aureus

COMPOSITE FAMILY

This Fleabane is a dwarf perennial that occurs in the alpine zone, growing on turf slopes. The deep green, oval leaves are on short stalks, and form a rosette on the ground. The yellow flowers have 25–70 ray florets, surrounding yellow disk florets, and appear singly on mostly leafless stems that grow up to 15 cm high. The bracts on the flower heads are covered with woolly hairs and have a purplish tip.

The origins of the common name, Fleabane, and the genus name, *Erigeron*, are discussed in the narrative on Daisy Fleabane (*E. compositus*), shown on page 48. Erigerons and Asters are often confused, but in the alpine elevations Erigerons usually bloom earlier than do Asters. Golden Fleabane might also be easily confused with Lyall's Ironplant (*Haplopappus lyallii*), shown on page 130, which occurs in the same habitat. Lyall's Ironplant has stalkless leaves (sessile), while Golden Fleabanes have stalked leaves.

Heart-Leaved Arnica
Arnica cordifolia

COMPOSITE FAMILY

Arnica is a common plant of wooded areas in the Rocky Mountains, foothills, and boreal forest. The leaves occur in 2–4 opposite pairs along the stem, each with long stalks and heart-shaped, serrated blades. The uppermost pair is stalkless, and more lance-shaped than the lower leaves. The flowers have 10–15 bright yellow ray florets, and bright yellow central disk florets.

Without careful dissection of the plant and examination under magnification, recognition of specific members of the genus *Arnica* can be difficult. The leaf structure on an individual plant is often the best clue to species recognition. The genus name, *Arnica*, is derived from the Greek *arnakis*, meaning "lamb's skin," a reference to the woolly bracts and leaf texture on many members of the genus. The species name, *cordifolia*, means "heart-shaped," a reference to the leaves of the plant. This species occasionally hybridizes with Mountain Arnica (*A. latifolia*) and the resulting hybrid can be difficult to identify. A number of Native peoples used Arnicas as a poultice for swellings and bruises. Arnicas are said to be poisonous if ingested.

Lyall's Ironplant (Lyall's Goldenweed)
Haplopappus lyallii

COMPOSITE FAMILY

This small perennial grows to heights of 15 cm from a taproot secured in meadows, scree slopes, and gravelly ridges in the alpine zone. The leaves are stemless, lance-shaped and hairy, glandular, and covered in a sticky coating. In addition, the leaves are clumped at the base of the flower stem, and extend up the stem. The yellow flower is a solitary composite head, with up to 35 ray flowers and yellow disk flowers.

Lyall's Ironplant was named in honour of David Lyall, a 19th-century Scottish botanist who collected a number of North American plants. This plant is often confused with Golden Fleabane (*Erigeron aureus*), shown on page 128, which occurs in the same habitat. However, Golden Fleabane does not have glands to give the leaves the sticky feel that is seen in Lyall's Ironplant. Golden Fleabane also has mainly basal leaves.

Slender Hawkweed
Hieracium gracile

COMPOSITE FAMILY

A plant common to open woods, meadows, roadsides, ditches, and disturbed areas. The yellow flower heads appear in a cluster on ascending stalks. The flowers are composed entirely of ray florets, no disk florets. The leaves are in a basal rosette, broadly lanced to spoon-shaped.

The genus name *Hieracium* is derived from the Greek *hierax*, meaning "hawk," as it was once believed that eating these plants improved a hawk's vision. The species name, *gracile*, means "slender." The leaves, stems, and roots produce a milky latex that was used as a chewing gum by British Columbia tribes. A similar species, Orange Hawkweed (*H. aurantiacum*), shown on page 161, occurs in similar habitat, but is usually found at lower elevations.

Spikelike Goldenrod

Solidago simplex (also *S. spathulata* and *S. decumbens*)

COMPOSITE FAMILY

This plant occurs at low to alpine elevations in dry areas, forest openings, and meadows. It can grow to heights of up to 80 cm, and has broadly lance- to spoon-shaped leaves which have hairless, toothed edges. The flowers occur in a dense, narrow, elongated cluster (raceme).

The origin of the genus name, *Solidago*, is explained in the narrative on Alpine Goldenrod (*S. multiradiata*), shown on page 123. It is a popular misconception that Goldenrods cause hay fever, but in fact, the pollen of the Goldenrods is too heavy to be easily carried on the wind—it must be carried from flower to flower by insects.

Bracted Lousewort (Wood Betony)
Pedicularis bracteosa

FIGWORT FAMILY

This plant can attain heights of up to a metre, and is found in subalpine and alpine elevations in moist forests, meadows, and clearings. The leaves are similar to those of ferns—divided into long, narrow, toothed segments—and are attached to the upper portions of the stem of the plant. The flowers vary in colour from yellow, to red, to purple. The flowers arise from the axils of leafy bracts, and occur in an elongated cluster at the top of the stem. The flowers have a two-lipped corolla, with the upper lip arched downwards and the lower lip curving upwards, giving the impression of a bird's beak.

The genus name, *Pedicularis*, is Latin for "louse," and plants of this genus are generally referred to as Louseworts. There was apparently a belief at one time that cattle that ate Louseworts were more likely to be afflicted by lice. The species name, *bracteosa*, refers to the leafy bracts below each flower. Louseworts are partially parasitic on the roots of other plants, and derive some of their nutrients from adjacent plants. Herbalists favour the plant as a sedative. The common name Betony is said to derive from an old Iberian word that meant "to cure all ills."

Yellow Beardtongue
Penstemon confertus

FIGWORT FAMILY

This is a plant of moist to dry meadows, woodlands, stream banks, hillsides, and mountains, and occurs from the prairie to the alpine zone. The small pale yellow flowers are numerous, and appear in whorled, interrupted clusters along the upper part of the stem. Each flower is tube shaped, and has 2 lips. The lower lip is three-lobed and bearded at the throat; the upper lip is two-lobed.

The common name, Beardtongue, describes the hairy, tongue-like staminode (sterile stamen) in the throat of the flower. The genus name, *Penstemon*, originates from the Greek *pente*, meaning "five," and *stemon*, meaning "stamen," five being the total number of stamens in the flower. The species name, *confertus*, is Latin meaning "crowded," a reference to the numerous flowers in the clusters. A number of Penstemons appear in Western Canada.

Yellow Monkeyflower
Mimulus guttatus

FIGWORT FAMILY

This plant occurs, often in large patches, along streams, seeps, and in moist meadows. The plant is quite variable, but always spectacular when found. The bright yellow flowers resemble Snapdragons, and occur in clusters. The flowers usually have red or purple dots on the lip, giving the appearance of a grinning face.

The genus name, *Mimulus*, is derived from the Latin *mimus*, meaning "mimic" or "actor," a reference to the "face" seen on the flower. The species name, *guttatus*, means "spotted" or "speckled." A related species, Red Monkeyflower, (*M. lewisii*), shown on page 168, is named in honour of Meriwether Lewis of the Lewis and Clark expedition, who collected the first specimen of the plant in 1805 near the headwaters of the Missouri River in Montana.

Golden Corydalis
Corydalis aurea

FUMITORY FAMILY

This plant of open woods, roadsides, disturbed places, and stream banks, is an erect or spreading, branched, leafy biennial or annual. It germinates in the fall and overwinters as a seedling. In the spring, it grows rapidly, flowers, and then dies. The yellow flowers are irregularly shaped, rather like the flowers of the Pea Family, with keels at the tips. A long, nectar-producing spur extends backwards from the upper petal.

The genus name, *Corydalis*, is derived from the Greek *korydallis*, meaning "crested lark," a reference to the spur of the petal resembling the spur of a lark. The species name, *aurea*, means "golden." Corydalis is generally considered poisonous because it contains isoquinoline and other alkaloids. Some poisoning of livestock has been reported. A similar species, Pink Corydalis (*C. sempervirens*), appears in similar habitat, but it has pink flowers with yellow tips, and is a taller and more erect plant.

Yellow Heather (Yellow Mountain Heather)
Phyllodoce glanduliflora

HEATH FAMILY

This is a dwarf evergreen shrub that grows up to 30 cm high, and thrives in subalpine and alpine meadows and slopes near timberline. The flowers, stems, and new growth are covered with small sticky hairs. The leaves are blunt, needle-like, and grooved on the undersides. The yellowish-green, vase- or urn-shaped flowers are nodding in clusters at the top of the stems.

The genus name, *Phyllodoce*, is explained in the note on Red Heather (*P. empetriformis*), shown on page 179. The species name, *glanduliflora*, refers to the glandular hairs that cover the plant and make it sticky. This plant is not a true heather, but it has been called by that name for so long that it might as well be. Red Heather and Yellow Heather occupy similar habitat, and they will hybridize to produce a variety of colours in the flowers.

Black Twinberry (Bracted Honeysuckle)
Lonicera involucrata

HONEYSUCKLE FAMILY

This plant is a shrub that grows up to 2 m tall in moist woods and along stream banks. The flowers are yellow and occur in pairs, arising from the axils of the leaves. The flowers are overlain by a purple to reddish leafy bract. As the fruit ripens, the bract remains, enlarges, and darkens in colour. The ripe fruits occur in pairs, and are black.

The genus name, *Lonicera*, honours the German botanist Adam Lonitzer. The species name, *involucrata*, refers to the prominent bracts. Some Native peoples believed that the Black Twinberries were poisonous, and would make one crazy. They are bitter to the taste, but serve as food for a variety of birds and small mammals.

Twining Honeysuckle
Lonicera dioica

HONEYSUCKLE FAMILY

A flowering vine of the Rocky Mountains, this plant clambers over low bushes and shrubs, and around tree trunks, at low to subalpine elevations. The trumpet-shaped flowers cluster inside a shallow cup formed by 2 leaves that are joined at their bases. The cupped leaves are very distinctive. When the flowers first open, they are yellow, turning orange to brick colour with age. The 5 petals are united into a funnel-shaped tube that has a swollen knob near the base where nectar is accumulated. Insects puncture the knob to obtain the sweet nectar. The flowers are very sweet scented. The fruits are small red berries, appearing in clusters.

The genus name, *Lonicera*, is to honour a 16th-century German botanist and physician, Adam Lonitzer. The common name, Honeysuckle, describes the sweet-tasting nectar of the flower. The stems of the Honeysuckles were woven into mats, bags, and blankets by various Native tribes.

Glacier Lily
Erythronium grandiflorum

LILY FAMILY

This gorgeous lily is one of the first blooms in the spring, often appearing at the edges of receding snowbanks on mountain slopes, thus the common name. The flowers are usually solitary, bright yellow, and nodding, with the sepals tapered to the tip and reflexed. The leaves, usually 2, are attached near the base of the stem, and are broadly oblong.

Erythronium is derived from the Greek *erythros*, meaning "red," referring to the red or pink flowers of some members of the genus. The species name, *grandiflorum*, means "large flowered." Also known locally as Avalanche Lily, Slide Lily, and Dogtooth Violet, Glacier Lilies are a favoured food of bears. Bears have been observed digging the yellow flowers and bulbs, then leaving them to wilt on the ground, returning days later to eat them. Evidently the bears are aware that the bulbs have an increased sweetness after being exposed to the air. Some Native peoples gathered the bulbs as a food source. The bulbs are inedible when raw, but prolonged steaming converts the indigestible carbohydrates into edible fructose. Drying the bulbs also helps in this process. Glacier Lilies often appear in large numbers, turning the hillsides yellow with their profusion.

Douglas Maple (Rocky Mountain Maple)
Acer glabrum

MAPLE FAMILY

This deciduous shrub or small tree is found in moist sheltered sites from foothills to subalpine zones. The plant has graceful, wide-spreading branches. The young twigs are smooth and cherry-red, turning grey with age. The leaves are opposite and typical of maples—three-lobed, with an unequal and sharp toothed margin. The yellowish-green flowers are short-lived and fragrant, with 5 petals and 5 sepals, hanging in loose clusters. The fruits are V-shaped pairs of winged seeds, joined at the point of attachment to the shrub. The fruit is known as a "samara."

Acer is Latin for "maple." The species name, *glabrum*, means "smooth, without hair." Native peoples had a variety of uses for this plant, including the manufacture of cordage, cradle frames, tepee pegs and joiners, bows, snowshoes, drum hoops, and fish traps.

Yellow Draba (Golden Whitlow Grass)
Draba aurea

MUSTARD FAMILY

This member of the Mustard Family grows up to 50 cm tall, and occurs on rocky slopes, in open woods, and in meadows from the montane to the alpine zones. The basal leaves are lance-shaped, hairy, and appear in a rosette. The stem leaves are stalkless, alternate, somewhat clasping on the stem, lance-shaped, hairy, and distributed up the stem. The flowers are four-petaled, bright yellow, and appear in a cluster at the top of the stem. Mustards typically have 4 petals in a cruciform shape. At one time the Mustard Family was known as *Cruciferae*, from the Latin *crux* or *crucis*, which means "cross."

The genus name, *Draba*, is derived from the Greek *drabe*, which means "acrid," a reference to the sap of some members of the Mustard Family. The species name, *aurea*, means "golden," a reference to the flower colour. Draba has traditionally been used to treat whitlow, a painful infection of the fingers that is caused by the herpes simplex virus, hence another common name, Yellow Whitlow Grass. Both common names are also applied to another related alpine species, *Draba paysonii*, which is a low-growing matted plant with numerous clusters of flowers. White Draba (*D. lonchocarpa*), also known as White Whitlow Grass, is also an alpine matting plant that has white flowers.

Soopolallie (Canadian Buffaloberry)
Shepherdia canadensis

OLEASTER FAMILY

This deciduous shrub grows up to 3 m tall, and is often the dominant under-story cover in lodgepole pine forests. All parts of the plant are covered with rust-coloured, shiny scales, giving the whole plant an orange, rusty appearance. The leaves are leathery and thick, green and glossy on the upper surface, while the lower surface is covered with white hairs, and sprinkled with rusty coloured dots. The plant is dioecious, that is, the male and female flowers appear on separate plants. The small inconspicuous yellow flowers often appear on the branches of the plant prior to the arrival of the leaves. The male flowers have 4 stamens, while the female flowers have none. In the fall, the female shrubs will be covered with small, translucent berries that are predominantly red.

The genus name, *Shepherdia*, is to honour the 18th-century English botanist John Shepherd. The common name, Soopolallie, is from the Chinook tribe— *soop* meaning "soap," and *olallie*, meaning "berry" —a reference to the fact that when beaten in water, the red berries produce a pink, soapy froth that some Native peoples liked to drink. The foam is derived from the bitter chemical saponins contained in the berries. Bears seem to relish the berries, and early settlers reported that buffalo browsed them, thus two of the common names. Other common names for the plant include Soapberry, Russet Buffaloberry, and Bearberry.

Pale Coralroot
Corallorhiza trifida

ORCHID FAMILY

A plant of moist woods and bogs, this orchid grows to heights of about 15 cm from extensive coral-like rhizomes. The plant is leafless, but has 2 or 3 bracts that sheath the stem. The yellow or greenish-yellow flowers are spread out along the thick, yellowish-green stalk, in a raceme towards the top of the stem. The flowers often have pale red dots on the lip.

The genus name, *Corallorhiza*, is derived from the Greek *korallion*, meaning "coral," and *rhiza*, meaning "root," a reference to the coral-shaped rhizomes from which the plant grows. The species name, *trifida*, is a reference to the three-lobed lip on the flower. All Coralroots are saprophytes, i.e., a plant that absorbs its nutrition from decaying organic matter and lacks any green pigment (chlorophyll) used by most plants for food production. This plant has some chlorophyll, enabling it to capture solar energy through photosynthesis, but it supplements that by parasitizing fungi in the soil. Two other Coralroots occur in the same habitat—the Striped Coralroot (*C. striata*), shown on page 188, and the Spotted Coralroot (*C. maculata*), shown on page 187. It is interesting to note that the Orchid Family is one of the largest plant families in the world, with over 400 genera and more than 20,000 species, most occurring in tropical regions.

Yellow Hedysarum
Hedysarum sulphurescens

PEA FAMILY

A plant of stream banks, grasslands, open forests, and clearings. The flowers are pea-like, yellowish to nearly white, drooping, and appear usually along one side of the stem in elongated clusters (racemes). The fruits of the plant are long, flattened, pendulous pods, with conspicuous winged edges, and constrictions between each of the seeds.

The genus name, *Hedysarum*, is derived from the Greek *hedys*, meaning "sweet," and *aroma*, meaning "smell." Yellow Hedysarum is also called Yellow Sweet Vetch. It is an extremely important food source for grizzly bears, which eat the roots in the spring and fall. A similar species, Alpine Hedysarum (*H. alpinum*), also known as Alpine Sweet Vetch, occurs in similar habitat. It has pink to purplish flowers.

Alpine Poppy
Papaver kluanensis

POPPY FAMILY

Alan Youell image

This is a dwarf replica of the popular garden denizen the Icelandic Poppy (*P. nudicaule*), but this one has yellow flowers, and lives on alpine shale slopes, rocky ledges, and screes high in the alpine zone. The leaves are numerous, basal, and finely dissected. The blades and stalks are covered with fine hairs. The plant grows in dense tufts from a perennial rootstock, and each plant can have several flower stalks. The flowers are bright yellow, with 4 or 5 petals, forming a cup. The flowers turn to pale green or brick red with age. The pistil and several united stigma form a star shape inside the petals. The fruit is a papery, oval capsule that is covered with long, brown bristles.

The genus name, *Papaver*, is the Latin name for "poppy." The species name, *kluanensis*, refers to Kluane, in the Yukon. The plant is rare in the Canadian Rocky Mountains.

Alpine Cinquefoil
Potentilla nivea

ROSE FAMILY

This dwarf perennial grows on exposed slopes and rocky crevices in the alpine zone. The leaves are basal, numerous, small, three-parted, and hug the ground in a dense cushion or mat. The leaves are silvery-green, and lightly hairy above, with dense coats of white hairs on the underside. The flowering stems are short, just lifting the yellow flowers above the leaves. The flowers have 5 petals and 5 sepals, with numerous stamens and pistils.

The origin of the genus name, *Potentilla*, is explained in the narrative on Shrubby Cinquefoil (*P. fruticosa*), shown on page 148. Alpine Cinquefoil lives in a very harsh environment, and the hairs on the plant help to reduce the intensity of sunlight, protect the plant from winds, and prevent excessive moisture loss.

Shrubby Cinquefoil
Potentilla fruticosa

ROSE FAMILY

This low deciduous shrub is found in dry meadows, on rocky slopes, and in gravelly river courses, at low to subalpine elevations. The leaves are alternate, divided into 3–7 (usually 5) leaflets that are lightly hairy, greyish-green, and often have curled edges. The flowers are golden yellow and saucer-shaped, with 5 rounded petals, usually blooming as a solitary at the end of branches. The flowers are often smaller and paler at lower elevations; larger and brighter at higher elevations.

The genus name, *Potentilla*, is derived from the Latin *potens*, meaning "powerful," most probably a reference to the supposed medicinal properties of the genus. The species name, *fruticosa*, means "shrubby," and refers to the plant forming a low, rounded bush, usually about a metre high. The common name is from the Latin *quinque*, meaning "five," and *folium*, meaning "leaf," a reference to the fact that many *Potentilla* species have 5 leaflets, and the flower parts are in fives. Shrubby Cinquefoil is a popular garden ornamental, and is easily propagated from cuttings.

Sibbaldia
Sibbaldia procumbens
ROSE FAMILY

This is a ground-hugging perennial that forms cushions in the alpine zone. The prostrate stems branch from the base, and terminate in clusters of 3 leaflets, similar to clover. These leaflets, however, are wedge-shaped, and each has 3 prominent teeth at the blunt end. White hairs cover both surfaces of the leaflets. The pale yellow flowers are generally saucer-shaped, and appear in clusters at the tops of the flowering stems. Each flower is made up of 5 yellow petals that alternate with 5 hairy, green sepals. The petals are about half as long as the sepals.

The genus name, *Sibbaldia*, honours Sir Robert Sibbald, an 18th-century Scottish physician and botanist. The species name, *procumbens*, means "prone or flat on the ground," a reference to the growth habit of the plant. Some confusion might arise if one encounters Sibbaldia in the same area as some member of the Cinquefoils (*Potentilla* spp). If the plant has 3 distinct teeth only at the end of the leaflets, it is Sibbaldia.

Yellow Mountain Avens
Dryas drummondii

ROSE FAMILY

A plant of gravelly streams and river banks, slopes and roadsides in the foothills and mountains. The yellow flower is solitary and nodding, with black, glandular hairs, blooming on the top of a hairy, leafless stalk. Leaves are alternate, leathery and wrinkly, dark green above and whitish-hairy beneath. The leaves are rounded at the tip, but wedge-shaped at the base. The margins are scalloped and slightly rolled under. The fruit consists of many achenes, each with a silky, golden yellow feathery plume, that becomes twisted around the others into a tight spiral, and later opens into a fluffy mass, dispersing the seeds on the wind.

The genus name, *Dryas,* was named for the Dryades, daughters of Zeus, the wood nymphs in Greek mythology. The species name, *drummondii*, honours Thomas Drummond, a Scottish naturalist who accompanied Franklin on his expedition to find the Northwest Passage. Some Native peoples used the plant for medicinal purposes, it being thought that it had healing properties for heart, kidney, and bladder trouble. This small flower likes calcium-rich soil, gravelly streams, and riverbanks, often creating large colonies of flowers. Another *Dryas*, White Mountain Avens or White Dryad (*D. octopetala*), shown on page 103, is abundant in the alpine zone, and it has eight-petaled white flowers with yellow stamens.

Yellow Mountain Saxifrage
Saxifraga aizoides

SAXIFRAGE FAMILY

Gill Ross image

This is a ground-hugging sturdy perennial that forms loose mats or cushions on moist sand, gravel, stream banks, and stones in the alpine zone. The upright stems are up to 10 cm tall, and are crowded with fat, succulent, linear leaves that have an abrupt tip. The leaves are covered in very small, pale hairs. The flowers appear at the tops of the stems, pale yellow, often spotted with orange. The flowers have 5 petals, which may be ragged at the tips. There are 10 stamens with conspicuously large anthers.

The origin of the genus name, *Saxifraga*, is explained in the note on Purple Saxifrage (*S. oppositifolia*), shown on page 32. The species name, *aizoides*, is derived from *aei*, meaning "always," and *zoon*, meaning "alive," a reference to the ability of this plant to survive in the bleak environment it inhabits.

Western St. John's Wort
Hypericum scouleri (also *H. formosum*)

ST. JOHN'S WORT FAMILY

Gill Ross image

This perennial appears in moist places from foothills to the alpine zone and grows to heights of 25 cm. The leaves are opposite, egg-shaped to elliptical, 1–3 cm long, somewhat clasping at the base, and usually have purplish-black dots along the edges. The bright yellow flowers have 5 petals and occur in open clusters at the top of the plant. The stamens are numerous and often look like a starburst.

The common name applied to members of this genus is a reference to St. John the Baptist. The spots on the leaves were said to ooze blood on the day of his execution. The genus name, *Hypericum*, is the Greek name for a European member of the genus. The species name, *scouleri*, honours John Scouler, a 19th-century Scottish physician and naturalist who collected plant specimens in western North America and the Galapagos Islands. A related species, Common St. John's Wort (*H. perforatum*) is a noxious European weed that has been introduced into North America and has spread across the continent at lower elevations. Plants in the genus contain compounds that are thought to be potent anti-viral agents, and the genus is being studied by AIDS researchers.

Common Stonecrop
Sedum lanceolatum
STONECROP FAMILY

Anne Elliott image

This fleshy perennial with reddish stems grows up to 15 cm tall on dry, rocky, open slopes, and in meadows and rock crevices from low elevations to above timberline. The leaves are numerous, round in cross-section, alternate, fleshy, overlapping, and mostly basal. The flowers are bright yellow, star-shaped with sharply pointed petals, and occur in dense, flat-topped clusters atop short stems.

The genus name, *Sedum*, is derived from the Latin *sedere*, which means "to sit," a reference to the plant's low-growing habit. The species name, *lanceolatum*, refers to the plant's lance-shaped leaves. The common name refers to the plant's normal habitat. Some authorities say the plant is edible, while others disagree. Roseroot (*S. rosea*), shown on page 193, is a related species that occurs in subalpine to alpine habitats, and has red flowers.

Round-Leaved Violet
Viola orbiculata

VIOLET FAMILY

This diminutive flower is an early bloomer, appearing right behind the melting snows in moist coniferous forests. The leaves lie flat on the ground, and are oval to nearly circular, often remaining green through the winter. The flowers are lemon yellow, and have purplish pencil marking on the lower 3 petals. The markings direct insects to the source of the nectar.

The species name *orbiculata* is a reference to the shape of the leaves. Candied flowers of this plant are often used for decorating cakes and pastries.

Yellow Wood Violet
Viola glabella
VIOLET FAMILY

This beautiful yellow violet occurs in moist woods, and often is found in extensive patches. The flowers tend to be a slightly larger size than Round-Leaved Violets (*V. orbiculata*), shown on page 154, and have somewhat shorter spurs.

The species name, *glabella*, is from "glabrous," meaning "smooth-skinned," a reference to the smooth leaves. The flower is also commonly referred to as Smooth Violet and Stream Violet.

Red, Orange, and Pink Flowers

This section contains flowers that are red, orange, or pink when encountered in the field. Flowers that are pinkish often can have tones running to lavender, so if you do not find the flower you are looking for, check the Blue/Purple section.

Mountain Sorrel
Oxyria digyna
BUCKWHEAT FAMILY

This relatively low-growing plant often appears in clumps at high elevations in moist rocky areas, along streams, and at lake margins in the subalpine and alpine zones. The leaves are often reddish in colour, primarily basal, smooth with wavy margins, and are distinctively kidney- or heart-shaped. The flowers appear in crowded clusters along several upright stems. The flowers are relatively inconspicuous, tiny, and green to reddish in colour. The fruits are flattened, papery, red seeds that have broad translucent wings.

The genus name, *Oxyria*, is derived from the Greek *oxys*, meaning "sour" or "sharp," a reference to the tart taste of the leaves. The common name, Sorrel, is said to originate from the Old High German word *sur*, meaning "sour." The plant is rich in vitamin C, and is said to be an antiscorbutic—a preventative for scurvy. A number of Native peoples used the plant as a food source. Mammals and birds also eat the plant.

Western Meadow Rue
Thalictrum occidentale

BUTTERCUP FAMILY

Western Meadow Rue is a dioecious species, which means that the male and female flowers are found on separate plants. The leaves on the plant are very similar in appearance to those of Columbines (*Aquilegia* ssp.), occurring in threes, but this plant's leaves are three times ternate—3 x 3 x 3—for a total of 27 leaflets per leaf. Neither gender of flowers has any petals. The male flower resembles a small wind chime, with the stamens hanging down like tassels. The female flowers resemble small, star-shaped pinwheels. The plant prefers cool, moist forest environments.

The genus name is derived from the Greek *thallo*, which means "to grow green," probably a reference to the bright green early shoots. The species name, *occidentale*, means "of the west." Native peoples used the plant variously as a medicine, as a love charm, and as a stimulant to horses. In modern times the plant is being investigated in chemotherapy research for cancer for its naturally occurring bioagents.

Wind Flower
Anemone multifida
BUTTERCUP FAMILY

This plant favours south-facing slopes, grasslands, and open woods. Like all anemones, Wind Flowers possess no petals, only sepals. The flowers are a variety of colours, from white, to yellowish, to red, and appear atop a woolly stem. Beneath the flowers are bract-like leaves attached directly to the stem. The leaves are palmate, with deeply incised, silky-haired leaflets, somewhat reminiscent of poppy leaves. The fruits are achenes in a rounded head, which later form a large cottony mass.

The common name, Wind Flower, comes from the method of distributing the long-plumed seeds of the plant. This flower is also commonly referred to as Cut-Leaved Anemone. A related species, Drummond's Anemone (*A. drummondii*), occurs in the alpine zone in the area. It has similar leaves to Wind Flower, but is generally smaller, and has whitish to bluish flowers.

Orange Agoseris (Orange Flowered False Dandelion)
Agoseris aurantiaca

COMPOSITE FAMILY

A common plant in moist to dry openings, meadows, and dry open forests in mid to alpine elevations. This plant is also known as False Dandelion, and occurs in both yellow (*A. glauca*) and orange. Agoseris shares many characteristics with the Dandelion (*Taraxacum officinale*), including a long taproot, a rosette of basal leaves, a leafless stem, a single flower appearing on a long stalk, and the production of a sticky, milky juice that is apparent when the stem is broken. Agoseris is generally a taller plant than Dandelion, its leaves are longer, and the leaf blades are smooth or faintly toothed, rather than deeply incised, as are Dandelion's. The bracts of the Agoseris flower heads are broader than Dandelion, and are never turned back along the stem, as they are in Dandelion.

Some Native peoples used the milky juice of the plant as a chewing gum. Infusions from the plant were also used for a variety of medicinal purposes.

Orange Hawkweed
Hieracium aurantiacum

VOMPOSITE FAMILY

A plant common to open woods, meadows, roadsides, ditches, and disturbed areas from low to subalpine areas, this conspicuous flower is an introduced species from Europe, where it has long been a garden ornamental. The species can spread rapidly and become a noxious weed. The orange flower heads appear in a cluster on ascending stalks. The flowers are composed entirely of ray florets, no disk florets. The leaves are in a basal rosette, broadly lanced to spoon-shaped.

The genus name, *Hieracium,* is derived from the Greek *hierax*, which means "hawk," as it was once believed that eating these plants improved a hawk's vision. The species name, *aurantiacum*, means "orange coloured." The leaves, stems, and roots produce a milky latex that was used as a chewing gum by British Columbia tribes. A yellow form of Hawkweed (*H. gracile*), shown on page 131, also appears in the same habitat as this plant.

Black Gooseberry (Swamp Currant)
Ribes lacustre

CURRANT FAMILY

An erect deciduous shrub, growing up to one and a half metres tall, that occurs in moist woods and open areas from foothills to the subalpine zone. The branches of the plant have small prickles and stout thorns at leaf and branch bases. The leaves are alternate and shaped like maple leaves, with 3–5 deeply cleft, palmate lobes. The flowers are reddish in colour, saucer-shaped, and hang in elongated clusters. The fruits are dark purple to black berries, which bristle with tiny hairs.

The genus name, *Ribes*, is derived from the Arabic *ribas*, the Moorish medical name for an unrelated rhubarb-like plant that grows in North Africa and Spain. The species name, *lacustre*, is derived from the Latin *lacus*, meaning "lake," or *lacustris*, meaning "inhabiting lakes." The genus includes all of the Currants and Gooseberries. This plant is also known as Bristly Black Currant. Commonly, members of the *Ribes* genus are divided into Currants and Gooseberries depending upon whether or not the berries are bristly hairy—Currants are not bristly hairy, and Gooseberries are. The spines on the plant can cause allergic reactions in some people.

Common Willowherb
Epilobium ciliatum (also *Epilobium glandulosum*)

EVENINGPRIMROSE FAMILY

This plant inhabits streamsides and wet areas in the montane and subalpine forest. Though it can grow over a metre tall, it is usually smaller. The leaves are opposite, lance-shaped, and clasp the stem, particularly near the base. The four-petaled flowers are white to purplish, with delicate purple markings. The petals are decidedly notched at the tip.

The genus name, *Epilobium*, is derived from the Greek *epi*, meaning "upon," and *lobos*, meaning "a pod," a reference to the inflorescence of plants of this genus occurring on top of the seed pod. The common name, Willowherb, is derived from the resemblance of their leaves to those of willows.

Fireweed
Epilobium angustifolium
EVENING PRIMROSE FAMILY

A plant of disturbed areas, roadsides, clearings, and shaded woods that occurs from low elevations to the subalpine zone. This plant is often one of the first plants to appear after a fire. The pink, four-petaled flowers bloom in long terminal clusters. Bracts between the petals are narrow. The flowers bloom from the bottom of the cluster first, then upward on the stem. The leaves are alternate and appear whorled.

The origin of the genus name, *Epilobium*, is explained in the narrative on Common Willowherb (*E. ciliatum*), shown on page 163. The species name, *angustifolium*, means "narrow-leafed." The common name originates from the plant's tendency to spring up from seeds and rhizomes on burned-over lands. The leaves resemble willow leaves, hence the alternate name Willowherb. The young leaves can be used in salads, and a weak tea can be brewed from the plant. The inner pith can be used to thicken soups and stews. Fireweed is the floral emblem of the Yukon.

River Beauty (Mountain Fireweed)
Epilobium latifolium

EVENING PRIMROSE FAMILY

Dennis Hall image

Also known as Dwarf Fireweed, this plant grows as a pioneer, often in dense colonies, on gravelly floodplains, and river bars, where the dense leaves and waving pink to purple flowers often obscure the stony ground underneath. River Beauty strongly resembles common Fireweed in appearance, but it has much shorter stems, broader leaves, and larger, more brilliantly coloured flowers. The large and showy, pink to rose-purple, four-petaled flowers bloom in a loose, short, leafy inflorescence. The leaves are bluish-green and waxy, with rounded tips.

The origin of the genus name, *Epilobium*, is explained in the narrative on Common Willowherb (*E. ciliatum*), shown on page 163. The species name, *latifolium*, means "broad-leafed." The young leaves can be used in salads, and a weak tea can be brewed from the plant. The inner pith can be used to thicken soups and stews. The plant is also cooling and astringent, and was used by some Native peoples to promote healing of wounds. Another related species, Alpine Willowherb (*E. anagallidifolium*) occurs in the area. That species is a low, mat-forming plant that appears in moist to wet rocky areas in the subalpine and alpine zones. The flowers are tiny, and may be pink to rose-coloured to white.

Elephant's Head
Pedicularis groenlandica

FIGWORT FAMILY

A plant of wet meadows, stream banks, and wetland margins. The flowers appear in dense clusters atop a substantial stalk which can reach 50 cm in height. Each of the flowers is reddish-purple to pinkish, and has an uncanny resemblance to an elephant's head, with a curved trunk and flared ears.

The origin of the genus name, *Pedicularis*, is explained in the narrative on Bracted Lousewort (*P. bracteosa*), shown on page 133. The species name, *groenlandica*, means "Greenland," though the learned references all seem to be in accord that the first specimens of the plant were found in Labrador, and nobody seems able to explain how Greenland got into the picture. All members of the genus are somewhat parasitic on the roots of other plants, so transplantation is doomed to failure. When encountered, a close examination of this delightful flower is recommended, but be careful of the fragile habitat in which it lives.

Paintbrush
Castilleja miniata
FIGWORT FAMILY

A plant of alpine meadows, well-drained slopes, open subalpine forests, moist stream banks, and open foothills woods. Paintbrush is widely distributed and extremely variable in colour—from pink, to red, to yellow, to white. The leaves are narrow and sharp-pointed, linear to lance-shaped, usually without teeth or divisions, but sometimes the upper leaves have 3 shallow lobes. The showy red, leafy bracts, which are actually modified leaves, resemble a brush dipped in paint, hence the common name.

The genus name, *Castilleja*, commemorates Domingo Castillejo, an 18th-century Spanish botanist. The species name, *miniata*, refers to the scarlet-red colour minium, an oxide of lead. Although beautiful, this plant should not be transplanted as it is partially parasitic and does not survive transplanting well.

Red Monkeyflower (Lewis's Monkeyflower)
Mimulus lewisii

FIGWORT FAMILY

This plant occurs, often in large patches, along mountain streams, and other moist areas in the subalpine and alpine zones. The leaves are clasping, opposite, conspicuously veined, and have irregular teeth along the margins. The showy red flowers arise from the axils of the upper leaves. The corolla is funnel-shaped, and has 2 lips. The upper lip is two-lobed and often bent backwards, and the lower lip is three-lobed, with hairs in the throat, and yellow markings on the lobes.

The genus name, *Mimulus*, is derived from the Latin *mimus*, meaning "mimic" or "actor," a reference to the "face" seen on the flower. The species name, *lewisii*, is in honour of Meriwether Lewis of the Lewis and Clark expedition, who collected the first specimen of the plant in 1805 near the headwaters of the Missouri River in Montana. Hummingbirds and bees are attracted to these flowers.

Thin-Leaved Owl's Clover
Orthocarpus tenuifolius

FIGWORT FAMILY

Owl's Clovers are very similar to the Paintbrushes (*Castillejas*), but the latter are mostly perennial, while the Owl's Clovers are annuals. In addition, the Paintbrushes have an upper floral lip that is much longer than the lower lip. In the Owl's Clovers, the upper floral lip is only slightly, if at all, longer than the lower lip.

The first botanical specimen of Thin-Leaved Owl's Clover was collected in 1806 by Meriwether Lewis on the banks of what was then called the Clark's River (now known as the Bitterroot River), while camped at a place called Travellers Rest. The Lewis and Clark expedition rested there after the exhausting crossing of the Bitterroot Mountains. The genus name, *Orthocarpus*, is derived from the Greek *orthos*, meaning "straight," and *karpos*, which means "fruit," a reference to the seed capsule of the plant.

Strawberry Blite
Chenopodium capitatum

GOOSEFOOT FAMILY

This plant is found from valley to subalpine elevations, and is distinctive for its large triangular or arrowhead-shaped leaves and its dense, fleshy clusters of bright red flowers. The flower clusters appear at the ends of branches on the plant, usually in interrupted bunches, and in the leaf axils.

The genus name, *Chenopodium*, is Greek for "goose foot," a reference to the leaf's resemblance to the foot of a goose. The leaves are rich in vitamins and minerals, and are said to taste like spinach. The flowers are edible, though most authorities warn against over-indulging in the plant. Some Native peoples used the red flowers as a dye, it being bright red initially, then darkening to purple as it ages. Another common name for the plant is Indian Paint.

Bog Cranberry
Vaccinium oxycoccos (also *Oxycoccus microcarpus*)
HEATH FAMILY

Glen Lee image

This plant is a creeping, vine-like, dwarf evergreen shrub that grows up to 40 cm tall in bogs and in wet sphagnum moss, from low to subalpine elevations. The stems are thin, wiry, and slightly hairy. The small leaves are alternate, leathery, sharp-pointed, and widely spaced on the stem. The leaves are dark green on the upper surface, lighter underneath, and the margins curl under. The nodding flowers are deep pink, with 4 petals that curve backwards exposing the stamens, reminiscent of the shape of Shooting Stars (*Dodecatheon pulchellum*), shown on page 31. The fruits are round red berries that appear disproportionately large for the tiny stems on which they hang.

The genus name, *Vaccinium*, is the Latin name for Blueberry. The species name, *oxycoccos*, is derived from the Greek *oxys*, meaning "acid, sharp or bitter," and *kokkos*, meaning "round berry," a reference to the tart taste of the fruits. The berries are high in vitamin C, and were used by Native peoples as a food source. Another Cranberry appears in the area—the Low-Bush Cranberry (*Viburnum edule*), shown on page 68—but it is a member of the Honeysuckle Family, and is a substantially different plant. There is another plant found at lower elevations that is also commonly known as Bog Cranberry (*V. vitis-idaea*), but it has larger, leathery leaves and white to pinkish urn-shaped flowers.

False Azalea (Fool's Huckleberry)
Menziesia ferruginea

HEATH FAMILY

This deciduous shrub is erect and spreading, and grows to heights of 2 m in moist wooded sites in the foothills to subalpine zones. The twigs of the shrub have fine, rust-coloured, sticky, glandular hairs, and give off a skunky odour when crushed. The leaves are alternate, elliptic, and broader above the middle. They are glandular hairy and have a prominent midvein protruding at the tip. The flowers are small, pinkish to greenish-orange, urn-shaped, and nodding on long, slender stalks. The flowers occur in clusters at the base of new growth. The fruit is a dark purplish capsule.

The genus name, *Menziesia*, honours Archibald Menzies, a physician and botanist who accompanied Captain George Vancouver in his northwest explorations in the late 18th century. The species name, *ferruginea*, is Latin meaning "iron rust," a reference to the rusty glands that cover the branches and the leaves. In the fall the leaves of the shrub take on very attractive orange and crimson colours. The common name False Azalea arises because the leaves of this plant resemble those of garden Azaleas. Another common name for the plant is Fool's Huckleberry, because the flowers might be mistaken for those of Huckleberries.

Grouseberry
Vaccinium scoparium
HEATH FAMILY

This low deciduous shrub grows up to 20 cm tall, and often forms dense ground cover on slopes in the foothills to subalpine zone. The branches are numerous, slender, and erect. The leaves are alternate, ovate, widest in the middle, and sharp-pointed, with finely serrated margins. The flowers are small, pinkish, urn-shaped, and nodding, hanging down singly from the leaf axils. The fruits are tiny, edible, bright red berries.

The Grouseberry is a member of the same genus as Blueberries, Huckleberries, and Cranberries. The species name, *scoparium*, is derived from the Latin *scopula*, meaning "broom-twig," a reference to the close, twiggy stems on the plant. The berries are very small, and some Native peoples gathered them using combs. Small mammals and birds eat the berries. Grouse eat all parts of the shrub, thus the common name Grouseberry.

Huckleberry
Vaccinium membranaceum

HEATH FAMILY

This erect, densely branched, deciduous shrub grows to heights of one and a half metres at mid to high elevations in dry to moist coniferous forests. The leaves are lance-shaped to elliptic, with pointed tips and finely toothed margins. The leaves turn red or purple in the fall. The flowers are creamy pink and urn-shaped, nodding on slender stalks. The fruits are black to dark purple berries 8–10 mm across.

Without question, the berry of this plant is among the most sought-after wild berries that occur in the Rocky Mountains—by human consumers, birds, and bears. The sweet taste of the berry is distinctive, and the berries are used to make jams, syrups, and liqueurs. Among those who harvest the berries, picking sites are jealously guarded. My son once asked a picker where he found the berries. The picker answered: "Sonny, I would sooner tell you that I was sleeping with your wife than I would where I pick Huckleberries!"

Kinnikinnick (Bearberry)
Arctostaphylos uva-ursi
HEATH FAMILY

This trailing or matted evergreen shrub grows low to the ground, and has long branches with reddish, flaky bark, and leathery, shiny green leaves. The flowers are pale pink and urn-shaped, appearing in clumps at the ends of the stems. The fruits are dull red berries.

The genus name, *Arctostaphylos*, is derived from the Greek *arktos*, meaning "bear," and *staphyle*, meaning "bunch of grapes." The species name, *uva-ursi*, is Latin for "bear's grape." The berries are apparently relished by bears and birds, though they tend to be dry and mealy to humans. They are edible and have been used as food, prepared in a variety of ways. The berries remain on the plant through the winter. One of the common names, Kinnikinnick, is believed to be of Algonquin origin, and means "something to smoke," a reference to the fact that some Native peoples used the leaves of the plant as a tobacco.

Pine-Drops

Pterospora andromedea

HEATH FAMILY

This purple or reddish-brown saprophyte (a plant that gets its nutrients from decaying plant or animal matter) stands up to a metre tall or more, and lives in deep humus of coniferous or mixed woods. The plants grow singly or in clusters, but they are rare. The leaves are mostly basal, and resemble scales. The stem stands erect, and is covered with glandular hairs. The flowers are cream-coloured to yellowish, and occur in a raceme that covers roughly the top half of the stalk. The petals are united into an urn shape, and hang downward off bent flower stalks, like small lanterns. The stalks of the plant will remain erect for a year or more after the plant dies.

The genus name, *Pterospora*, is derived from the Greek *pteron*, meaning "wing," and *sporos*, meaning "seed," a reference to the winged appearance of the seeds. The species name, *andromedea*, refers to Andromeda of Greek mythology. To review the story of Andromeda, see White Heather (*Cassiope mertensiana*), shown on page 65. I am at a complete loss as to how the taxonomist connected this plant to that particular myth, and I have so far been unable to explain the connection.

Pink Wintergreen
Pyrola asarifolia

HEATH FAMILY

An erect perennial that inhabits moist to dry coniferous and mixed forests, and riverine environments, from the montane to the subalpine zone. The flowers are shaped like an inverted cup or bell, nodding, waxy, pale pink to purplish-red, and have a long, curved, projecting style. The leaves are basal in a rosette. The leaves have a leathery appearance, and are shiny, rounded, and dark green.

The origin of the genus name, *Pyrola*, is explained in the narrative on Greenish Flowered Wintergreen (*P. chlorantha*), shown on page 60. The species name, *asarifolia*, is derived from the Latin *asarum*, meaning "ginger," and *folium*, meaning "leaf," a reference to the similarity between the leaves of this plant and those of wild ginger. They are called wintergreen, not because of the taste, but because the leaves remain green during the winter. Like orchids, many of these plants require a specific fungus in the soil to grow successfully, and transplantation should not be attempted. Two other species of *Pyrola*, Greenish Flowered Wintergreen and One-Sided Wintergreen (*P. secunda*), shown on page 62, occur in similar habitat.

Prince's-Pine (Pipsissewa)
Chimaphila umbellata

HEATH FAMILY

This small evergreen shrub grows to heights of 30 cm in coniferous woods. The dark green, glossy leaves are narrowly spoon-shaped, saw-toothed, and occur in whorls. The flowers are pink, waxy, saucer-shaped, and nodding on an erect stem above the leaves. The fruits of the plant are dry, round, brown capsules that often overwinter on the stem.

The genus name, *Chimaphila*, is derived from the Greek *cheima*, meaning "winter," and *philos*, meaning "loving," descriptive of the evergreen leaves. Prince's-Pine is also known as Pipsissewa, an adaptation of the Cree name for the plant—*pipisisikweu*—meaning "it breaks into small pieces," a reference to a substance in the leaves that was said to dissolve kidney and gall stones. The plant was often used to make a medicinal tea. Both Native peoples and settlers to North America used the plant for a variety of medicinal purposes.

Red Heather (Red Mountain Heather)
Phyllodoce empetriformis

HEATH FAMILY

This dwarf evergreen shrub grows up to 30 cm tall, and thrives in subalpine and alpine meadows and slopes near timberline. The leaves are blunt, needle-like, and grooved on both sides. The red to pink, urn-shaped flowers are erect and/or nodding in clusters at the top of the stems.

The genus name, *Phyllodoce*, appears to honour a sea-nymph from Greek mythology, but none of the learned authorities seem to know why that mythical character is associated with this genus. The species name, *empetriformis*, also is the source of controversy. Some authorities say the name arises because the leaves of this plant resemble those of the genus *Empetrum*—the Crowberry Family. Other authorities say the species name is derived from the Greek *en*, meaning "on," and *petros*, meaning "rocks," a reference to the rocky habitat favoured by the plant. This plant is not a true heather, but it has been called by that name for so long that it might as well be. The first sample of the plant was collected by Lewis and Clark during their expedition, but the exact location of its collection has been lost.

Swamp Laurel
Kalmia microphylla

HEATH FAMILY

This low-growing evergreen shrub occurs in cool bogs, on stream banks, and lakeshores in the subalpine and alpine zones. The leaves are leathery, dark green above and greyish white beneath, often with the margins rolled under. The flowers are pink to rose-coloured, with the petals fused together to form a saucer or bowl, appearing on a reddish stalk. There are 10 purple-tipped stamens protruding from the petals.

The genus name, *Kalmia*, is to honour Peter Kalm, a student of Carolus Linnaeus at Uppsala University in Sweden. Linnaeus was a prominent botanist who developed binomial nomenclature for plants. The leaves and flowers of this plant contain poisonous alkaloids that can be fatal to humans and livestock if ingested.

Twinflower
Linnaea borealis
HONEYSUCKLE FAMILY

This small trailing evergreen is common in coniferous forests, but easily overlooked by the casual observer. This plant sends runners creeping over the forest floor, over mosses, fallen logs, and stumps. At frequent intervals the runners give rise to the distinctive "Y" shaped stems, 5–10 cm tall. Each fork of the stem supports at its end a slightly flared, pink to white, trumpet-like flower that hangs down like a small lantern on a tiny lamppost. The flowers have a sweet perfume that is most evident near evening.

The genus name, *Linnaea*, honours Carolus Linnaeus, the Swedish botanist who is the father of modern plant nomenclature. It is said that this flower was his favourite among the thousands of plants he knew. The species name, *borealis*, means "northern," referring to the circumpolar northern habitat of the plant. Some Native peoples made a tea from the leaves of this plant.

Nodding Onion
Allium cernuum

LILY FAMILY

All *Allium* species smell strongly of onion, and have small flower clusters at the top of the leafless stalk. Nodding Onion is the most common species in the Rocky Mountain region, and is easily identified by its pink drooping or nodding inflorescence.

The stem gives off an oniony odour when crushed, and is said to be one of the better tasting wild onions. Native peoples gathered the bulbs and ate them raw and cooked; used them for flavouring other foods; and dried them for later use. Bears and ground squirrels also use this plant in their diets. *Allium* is the Latin name for "garlic," from the Celtic *all*, meaning "hot" or "burning," because it irritates the eyes. The species name, *cernuum*, refers to the crook in the stem of the plant just below the flower.

Tiger Lily
Lilium columbianum

LILY FAMILY

True lilies are recognized by their large, showy flowers, smooth, unbranched stems, and whorls of narrow, lance-shaped leaves. Tiger Lily can have up to 30 flowers per stem. The orange to orange-yellow flowers are downward-hanging, with curled-back petals, and deep red to purplish spots near the centre. The flowers are very similar to Western Wood Lily (*L. philadelphicum*), shown on page 184, but the Wood Lily petals form more of a chalice shape, without the petals curling back like those of the Tiger Lily.

The common name for the Tiger Lily most probably comes from the spotting on the petals. There was once a superstition that smelling the Tiger Lily would give you freckles. The bulbs of Tiger Lily were used as food by Native tribes, and were said to have a peppery taste, and would add a peppery taste to other foods. Like other lilies, this one will die if the flower is picked. The bulb depends upon the flower for nutrients, and if the flower is removed, the bulb will starve and die.

Western Wood Lily
Lilium philadelphicum (also *Lilium umbellatum*)

LILY FAMILY

This lily grows in moist meadows, dense to open woods, and edges of aspen groves, from prairie elevations to the low subalpine zone. The leaves are numerous, lance-shaped, smooth, and alternate on the stem, except for the upper leaves, which are in whorls. Each plant may produce from 1–5 bright orange to orange-red flowers, each with 3 petals and 3 similar sepals. The petals and the sepals are orange at the tip, becoming yellowish and black, or purple-dotted, at the bases. The anthers are dark purple in colour.

Lilium is the Latin name for the plant. There are several stories as to how the species name originates. One explanation holds that Linnaeus—the Swedish naturalist who invented binominal identification for plants—received his specimens of the plant from a student in Philadelphia. Another explanation holds that the name comes from the Greek words *philos*, meaning "love," and *delphicus*, the ancient wooded oracle at Delphi, hence "wood lover." The Western Wood Lily is the floral emblem of Saskatchewan, but it is becoming increasingly rare, owing to picking of the flower. The bulb from which the flower grows depends upon the flower for nutrients, and will die if the flower is picked. The plants do not survive transplantation well, but can be grown from seeds, though the propagated plants might not flower for several years. The bulbs were eaten by some Native tribes, but were generally considered to be bitter. The Blackfoot treated spider bites with a wet dressing of the crushed flowers. Western Wood Lily is often confused with Tiger Lily (*L. columbianum*), shown on page 183, which are coloured similarly, but the petals on the Tiger Lily are curled backwards, while the petals on the Wood Lily are held in a chalice shape.

Mountain Hollyhock
Iliamna rivularis

MALLOW FAMILY

This large plant can grow up to 2 m tall, and appears in montane to sub-alpine elevations on moist slopes, stream banks, and meadows. The leaves are fairly large, alternate, irregularly toothed, and resemble maple leaves, with 5–7 lobes each. The relatively large, pink to whitish, saucer-shaped flowers resemble garden Hollyhocks. They appear from the leaf axils along the stem and at the tips of the stems, in long, interrupted clusters. The flowers have many stamens, the filaments of which are united at the base to form a tube.

The derivation of the genus name, *Iliamna*, is unknown, though some authorities suggest that it honours Rhea Sylvia (also known as Ilia), the mythological mother of Romulus and Remus, the twins who are said to have founded Rome. The species name, *rivularis*, is derived from Latin and means "of the brook," a reference to the plant's favoured habitat. Mountain Hollyhock is an early succession plant following a forest fire.

Alpine Wallflower
Erysimum pallasii

MUSTARD FAMILY

Cleve Wershler image

This little beauty inhabits dry, rocky terrain in the alpine zone. The leaves are long, prominently veined, and deeply notched, arrayed in a rosette on the ground. The numerous sweet-scented flowers are purple and cruciform-shaped, nestling on short stems inside the rosette of leaves. The flowering stems elongate after fertilization to become long, curved, purple seed pods.

According to most authorities the genus name, *Erysimum*, is derived from the Greek *eruein*, meaning "to draw," a reference to the fact that the acrid juices of mustard-based poultices were thought to draw out the cause of pain. The origin of the species name is vague, but most probably it honours Peter Pallas, an 18th-century botanist at the Swedish Museum of Natural History.

Spotted Coralroot
Corallorhiza maculata

ORCHID FAMILY

A plant of moist woods and bogs, this orchid grows from extensive coral-like rhizomes. There are no leaves, but the plant has several membranous bracts that sheath the purplish to brownish stem. A number of flowers appear on each stem, loosely arranged up the stem in a raceme. The 3 sepals and 2 upper petals are reddish purple. The lip petal is white, with dark red or purple spots, and 2 lateral lobes.

The origin of the genus name, *Corallorhiza*, is explained in the narrative on Pale Coralroot (*C. trifida*), shown on page 144. Lacking chlorophyll, this plant does not produce food by photosynthesis, but rather through parasitizing fungi in the soil. Two other Coralroots occur in the same habitat as the Spotted—the Pale Coralroot and the Striped Coralroot (*C. striata*), shown on page 188.

Striped Coralroot
Corallorhiza striata

ORCHID FAMILY

A plant of moist woods and bogs, this orchid grows from extensive coral-like rhizomes, and occurs in the montane and subalpine zones. The pink to yellowish-pink flowers have purplish stripes on the sepals, and the lowest petal forms a tongue-shaped lip. A number of flowers appear on each stem, loosely arranged up the stem in an unbranched raceme. The leaves are tubular sheaths that surround, and somewhat conceal, the base of the purplish stem

The origin of the genus name, *Corallorhiza*, is explained in the note on Pale Coralroot (*C. trifida*), shown on page 144. Two other Coralroots occur in the same habitat as the Striped—the Pale Coralroot and the Spotted Coralroot (*C. maculata*), shown on page 187. Of the three, the Striped Coralroots have the largest flowers. Striped Coralroot is sometimes referred to as Madder-Stripes. The coralroots depend on a complex relationship with fungi in the soil for germination and survival.

Venus Slipper

Calypso bulbosa

ORCHID FAMILY

An orchid found in shaded, moist coniferous forests. The flowers are solitary and nodding on leafless stems. The flower has pinkish to purplish sepals, and mauve side petals. The lip is whitish or purplish, with red to purple spots or stripes, and is hairy yellow inside. The flower is on the top of a single stalk, with a deeply wrinkled appearance. This small but extraordinarily beautiful flower blooms in the early spring, often occurring in colonies.

The Venus Slipper has many common names, including Fairy Slipper and Calypso Orchid. The genus name, *Calypso*, is derived from Greek mythology, Calypso being the daughter of Atlas. *Calypso* means "concealment," and is very apt, given that this flower is very easy to miss, being small, delicate, and growing in out-of-the-way places. The species name, *bulbosa*, refers to the bulb-like corm from which the flower grows. Do not attempt to transplant this flower. It needs specific fungi in the soil to grow successfully. Its range has diminished over time, owing to over-picking.

Alpine Milk-Vetch
Astragalus alpinus

PEA FAMILY

This plant arises from creeping rhizomes and forms mats in mid to alpine elevations in moist thickets, on gravel bars, in lake margins, and on scree slopes. The leaves are pinnately compound, with 13–23 oval to elliptic, hairy leaflets. The flowers are borne in dense clusters at the ends of the stems. The flowers are pea-like, and two-toned in colour—the standard and tip of the keel are pale blue or violet, and the wings are white. The fruits of the plant are brown, hanging pods that are covered with black hairs.

The origin of the genus name appears to be in some doubt. Some authorities say it is a reference to an Old World plant, the specifics of which have been lost. Others say it is derived from a Greek word that means "ankle bone," and is a reference to the pod shape of some members of the genus. This plant is also known as Mountain Locoweed. Native peoples extracted a yellow dye from the flowers, leaves, and stems of these plants.

Moss Campion
Silene acaulis

PINK FAMILY

This low-growing, ground-hugging cushion plant occupies an alpine environment in rock crevices, on cliffs, and exposed ridges. The bright green, narrow leaves are linear to narrowly lance-shaped, arise from the base of the plant, and often form cushions up to a metre in diameter, resembling moss. Dead leaves from previous seasons often persist for years. The small, pink, five-lobed, tubular flowers are borne on single, short stalks, but they often appear to be sitting on the mossy surface.

While this is an alpine species, it is often grown in rock gardens, and is easily propagated from seeds. The species name, *acaulis*, means "not stalked," a reference to the stalkless appearance of the flowers. This plant might be confused with Moss Phlox (*Phlox hoodii*), but Moss Phlox occurs at much lower elevations and not in the alpine environment.

Dwarf Raspberry (Arctic Raspberry)
Rubus arcticus (also *R. acaulis*)

ROSE FAMILY

Anne Elliott image

This plant is a low, creeping, dwarf shrub that grows from a trailing rootstock, and is most often found in wet meadows and around seeps in the subalpine and alpine zones. The leaves are divided into 3 leaflets that are round to heart-shaped, and have coarsely toothed edges. The flowers are usually solitary, pink and five-petaled. The fruits are clusters of red drupelets, the aggregate of which is the raspberry. The fruits are small, but are sweet and flavourful.

The genus name, *Rubus*, is Latin, meaning "red," a reference to the colour of the fruits. The berries have long been used as a food source, and some Native peoples used them to concoct a tea. The plant is also locally known as Dwarf Nagoonberry, but the origin of that name is unknown.

Roseroot

Sedum rosea (also *Tolmachevia integrifolia*)

STONECROP FAMILY

This is a fairly rare plant that occurs in the subalpine and alpine zones, favouring moist rocky scree, talus, and ridges. The stems arise from a fleshy rootstock, and they are covered in persistent leaves. The leaves are oval to oblong, fleshy, and somewhat flattened. The flowers have oblong petals, are rose-coloured to purple, and occur in rounded, flat-topped, dense clusters atop the stems.

When the roots are cut or bruised, they give off the fragrance of roses, thus the common name. Another common name is King's Crown, a reference to the shape of the inflorescence. Some Native peoples used Roseroot medicinally in poultices.

GLOSSARY

Achene: A dry, single-seeded fruit that does not split open at maturity

Alkaloid: Any of a group of complex, nitrogen-based chemicals, often found in plants, that are thought to protect the plants against insect predation. Many of these substances are poisonous

Alternate: A reference to the arrangement of leaves on a stem where the leaves appear singly and staggered on opposite sides of the stem

Annual: A plant that completes its life cycle, from seed germination to production of new seed, within a year and then dies

Anther: The portion of the stamen (the male portion of a flower) that produces pollen

Axil: The upper angle formed where a leaf, branch, or other organ is attached to a plant stem

Basal: A reference to leaves that are found at the base or bottom of the plant, usually near ground level

Berry: A fleshy, many-seeded fruit

Biennial: A plant that completes its life cycle in two years, normally producing leaves in the first year, but not producing flowers until the second year, then dies

Blade: The body of a leaf, excluding the stalk

Bract: A reduced or otherwise modified leaf that is usually found near the flower or inflorescence of a plant, but is not part of the flower or inflorescence

Bristle: A stiff hair, usually erect or curving away from its attachment point

Bulb: An underground plant part derived from a short, often rounded shoot that is covered with scales or leaves

Calcareous: In reference to soils, containing calcium carbonate

Calyx: The outer set of flower parts, usually composed of sepals

Capsule: A dry fruit with more than one compartment that splits open to release seeds

Clasping: In reference to a leaf, surrounding or partially wrapping around a stem or branch

Cluster: A grouping or close arrangement of individual flowers that is not dense and continuous

Composite inflorescence: A flower-like inflorescence of the Composite Family, composed of ray and/or disk flowers. Where both ray and disk flowers are present, the ray flowers surround the disk flowers

Compound leaf: A leaf that is divided into two or many leaflets, each of which may look like a complete leaf, but which lacks buds. Compound leaves may have a variety of arrangements. Pinnate leaves have leaflets arranged like a feather, with attachment to a central stem. Palmate leaves have leaflets radiating from a common point, like the fingers of a hand

Corm: An enlarged base or stem resembling a bulb

Corolla: The collective term for the petals of the flower that are found inside the sepals

Cultivar: A cultivated variety of a wild plant

Cyme: A broad, flat-topped flower arrangement in which the inner, central flowers bloom first

Decumbent: In reference to a plant, reclining or lying on the ground, with tip ascending

Decurrent: In reference to a leaf, extending down from the point of insertion on the stem, so when the edges of the leaf continue down the stem, they form wings on the stem

Disk flower: Any of the small tubular florets found in the central clustered portion of the flower head of members of the Composite Family; also referred to as "disk florets"

Dioecious: Having unisex flowers, where male and female flowers appear on separate plants; see *monoecious*

Drupe: A fleshy or juicy fruit that covers a single, stony seed inside, e.g., a cherry or peach

Drupelet: Any one part of an aggregate fruit (like a raspberry or blackberry), where each such part is a fleshy fruit that covers a single, stony seed inside

Elliptic: Ellipse-shaped, widest in the middle

Elongate: Having a slender form, long in relation to width

Entire: In reference to a leaf, a leaf edge that is smooth, without teeth or notches

Filament: The part of the stamen that supports the anther. Also can refer to any threadlike structure

Florescence: Generally the flowering part of a plant; the arrangement of the flowers on the stem; also referred to as "inflorescence"

Floret: One of the small tubular flowers in the central, clustered portion of the flower head of members of the Composite Family; also known as "disk flower"

Flower head: A dense and continuous group of flowers without obvious branches or spaces between

Follicle: A dry fruit composed of a single compartment that splits open along one side at maturity to release seeds

Fruit: The ripe ovary with the enclosed seeds, and any other structures that enclose it

Gland: A small organ that secretes a sticky or oily substance, and is attached to some part of the plant

Glandular hairs: Small hairs attached to glands on plants

Glaucous: With a fine, waxy, often white coating that may be rubbed off; often characteristic of leaves, fruits, and stems

Hood: in reference to flower structure, a curving or folded, petal-like structure interior to the petals and exterior to the stamens in certain flowers

Host: In reference to a parasitic or semi-parasitic plant, the plant from which the parasite obtains its nourishment

Inflorescence: Generally the flowering part of a plant; the arrangement of the flowers on the stem; also referred to as "florescence"

Involucral bract: A modified leaf found just below an inflorescence

Keel: A ridge or fold, shaped like the bottom of a boat, which may refer to leaf structure, or more often to the two fused petals in flowers that are members of the Pea Family

Lance-shaped: In reference to leaf shape, much longer than wide, widest below the middle and tapering to the tip, like the blade of a lance

Leaflet: A distinct, leaflike segment of a compound leaf

Linear: Like a line; long, narrow, and parallel-sided

Lobe: A reference to the arrangement of leaves, a segment of a divided plant part, typically rounded

Margin: The edge of a leaf or petal

Mat: A densely interwoven or tangled, low, ground-hugging growth

Midrib: The main rib of a leaf

Midvein: The middle vein of a leaf

Monoecious: A plant having unisex flowers, with separate male and female flowers on the same plant; see *dioecious*

Nectary: A plant structure that produces and secretes nectar

Node: A joint on a stem or root

Noxious weed: A plant, usually imported, that out-competes and drives out native plants

Oblong: Somewhat rectangular, with rounded ends

Obovate: Shaped like a teardrop

Opposite: A reference to the arrangement of leaves on a stem where the leaves appear paired on opposite sides of the stem, directly across from each other

Oval: Broadly elliptic

Ovary: The portion of the flower where the seeds develop. It is usually a swollen area below the style and stigma

Ovate: Egg shaped

Palmate: A reference to the arrangement of leaves on a stem where the leaves spread like the fingers on a hand, diverging from a central or common point

Panicle: A branched inflorescence that blooms from the bottom up

Pappus: The cluster of bristles, scales, or hairs at the top of an achene in the flowers of the Composite Family

Pencilled: Marked with coloured lines, like the petals on Violets

Perennial: A plant that does not produce seeds or flowers until its second year of life, then lives for three or more years, usually flowering each year before dying

Petal: A component of the inner floral portion of a flower, often the most brightly coloured and visible part of the flower

Petiole: The stem of a leaf

Pinnate: A reference to the arrangement of leaves on a stem where the leaves appear in two rows on opposite sides of a central stem, similar to the construction of a feather

Pistil: The female member of a flower that produces seed, consisting of the ovary, the style, and the stigma. A flower may have one to several separate pistils

Pistillate: A flower with female reproductive parts, but no male reproductive parts

Pod: A dry fruit

Pollen: The tiny, often powdery, male reproductive microspores formed in the stamens and necessary for sexual reproduction in flowering plants

Pome: A fruit with a core, e.g., an apple or pear

Prickle: A small, sharp, spiny outgrowth from the outer surface

Raceme: A flower arrangement that has an elongated flower cluster with the flowers attached to short stalks of relatively equal length that are attached to the main central stalk

Ray flower: One of the outer strap-shaped petals seen in members of the Composite Family. Ray flowers may surround disk flowers or may comprise the whole of the flower head; also referred to as "ray florets"

Reflexed: Bent backwards, often in reference to petals, bracts, or stalks

Rhizome: An underground stem that produces roots and shoots at the nodes

Riverine: Moist habitats along rivers or streams

Rootstock: Short, erect, underground stem, from which new leaves and shoots are produced annually

Rosette: A dense cluster of basal leaves from a common underground part, often in a flattened, circular arrangement

Runner: A long, trailing or creeping stem

Saprophyte: An organism that obtains its nutrients from dead organic matter

Sepal: A leaf-like appendage that surrounds the petals of a flower. Collectively the sepals make up the calyx

Serrate: Possessing sharp, forward-pointing teeth

Sessile: Of leaves, attached directly to the base, without a stalk

Shrub: A multi-stemmed woody plant

Simple leaf: A leaf that has a single leaf-like blade, which may be lobed or divided

Spike: An elongated, unbranched cluster of stalkless or nearly stalkless flowers

Spine: A thin, stiff, sharp-pointed projection

Spur: A hollow, tubular projection arising from the base of a petal or sepal, often producing nectar

Spurred corolla: A corolla that has spurs

Stalk: The stem supporting the leaf, flower, or flower cluster

Stamen: The male member of the flower that produces pollen, typically consisting of an anther and a filament

Staminate: A flower with male reproductive parts, but no female reproductive parts

Staminode: A sterile stamen

Standard: The uppermost petal of a typical flower in the Pea Family

Stigma: The portion of the pistil receptive to pollination; usually at the top of the style, and often sticky or fuzzy

Stipule: An appendage, usually in pairs, found at the base of a leaf or leaf stalk

Stolon: A creeping, above-ground stem capable of sending up a new plant

Style: A slender stalk connecting the stigma to the ovary in the female organ of a flower

Talus: Loose, fragmented rock rubble usually found at the base of a rock wall, also known as "scree"

Taproot: A stout main root that extends downward

Tendril: A slender, coiled, or twisted filament with which climbing plants attach to their supports

Tepals: Petals and sepals that cannot be distinguished from one another

Terminal flower head: A flower that appears at the top of a stem, as opposed to originating from a leaf axil

Ternate: Arranged in threes, often in reference to leaf structures

Toothed: Bearing teeth or sharply angled projections along the edge

Trailing: Lying flat on the ground, but not rooting

Tuber: A thick, creeping, underground stem

Tubular: Hollow or cylindrical, usually in reference to a fused corolla

Umbel: A flower arrangement where the flower stalks have a common point of attachment to the stem, like the spokes of an umbrella

Unisexual: Some flowers are unisexual, having either male parts or female parts, but not both. Some plants are unisexual, having either male flowers or female flowers, but not both

Urn-shaped: Hollow and cylindrical or globular, contracted at the mouth; like an urn

Vacuole: A membrane-bound compartment in a plant that is typically filled with liquid, and may perform various functions in the plant

Vein: A small tube that carries water, nutrients, and minerals, usually in reference to leaves

Whorl: Three or more parts attached at the same point along a stem or axis, often surrounding the stem; forming a ring radiating out from a common point

Wings: Side petals that flank the keel in typical flowers of the Pea Family

PLANT FAMILIES ARRANGED ACCORDING TO COLOUR

BLUE & PURPLE FLOWERS

Bladderwort Family
    Common Butterwort
Bluebell Family
    Kalm's Lobelia
Borage Family
    Blueweed
    Stickseed
    Tall Lungwort (Mertensia)
Buttercup Family
    Blue Clematis
    Blue Columbine
    Low Larkspur
    Prairie Crocus
Composite Family
    Blue Lettuce
    Bull Thistle
    Canada Thistle
    Common Burdock
    Parry's Townsendia
    Showy Aster
    Smooth Blue Aster
    Smooth Fleabane
Figwort Family
    Lilac-Flowered Beardtongue
    Small-Flowered Beardtongue
    Smooth Blue Beardtongue
Flax Family
    Blue Flax
Four-O'Clock Family
    Hairy Four-O'Clock
    (Umbrellawort)
Gentian Family
    Northern Gentian
Oblong-Leaved Gentian
    (Prairie Gentian)
Geranium Family
    Sticky Purple Geranium
Harebell Family
    Harebell
Heath Family
    Western Bog-Laurel
    (Swamp Laurel)

Iris Family
    Blue-Eyed Grass
Mint Family
    Giant Hyssop
    Heal-All (Self-Heal)
    Marsh Hedge-Nettle
    Marsh Skullcap
    Wild Mint (Canada Mint)
Mustard Family
    Dame's Rocket (Dame's Violet)
Orchid Family
    Spotted Coralroot
    Striped Coralroot
    Venus Slipper
Pea Family
    Ascending Purple Milk-Vetch
    Indian Breadroot
    Purple Milk-Vetch
    Purple Prairie-Clover
    Showy Locoweed
    Silky Lupine
    Two-Grooved Milk-Vetch
Primrose Family
    Shooting Star
Rose Family
    Purple Avens
Violet Family
    Bog Violet
    Crowfoot Violet (Prairie Violet)
    Early Blue Violet
Waterleaf Family
    Thread-Leaved Phacelia
    (Thread-Leaved
      Scorpionweed)

RED, ORANGE & PINK FLOWERS

Borage Family
    Common Hound's-Tongue
Buckwheat Family
    Water Smartweed
Buttercup Family
    Red Columbine

Cactus Family
    Cushion Cactus (Ball Cactus)
Caper Family
    Bee Plant
Composite Family
    Dotted Blazingstar
    Flodman's Thistle
    Spotted Knapweed
Currant Family
    Black Gooseberry
Evening Primrose Family
    Fireweed
    Scarlet Butterflyweed
Figwort Family
    Paintbrush
Goosefoot Family
    Strawberry Blite
Heath Family
    Kinnikinnick (Bearberry)
    Pine-Drops
    Pink Wintergreen
Lily Family
    Nodding Onion
    Western Wood Lily
Mallow Family
    Scarlet Mallow
Milkweed Family
    Showy Milkweed
Mint Family
    Wild Bergamot
Pea Family
    Red Clover
Pitcher Plant Family
    Pitcher Plant
Primrose Family
    Sea Milkwort
Rose Family
    Prickly Rose
    Three-Flowered Avens
      (Old Man's Whiskers,
      Prairie Smoke)

WHITE, GREEN & BROWN FLOWERS
Arum Family
    Water Calla (Water Arum)
Blazing Star Family
    Evening Star
Borage Family
    Clustered Oreocarya
Buck-Bean Family
    Buck-Bean (Bog-Bean)
Buckwheat Family
    Narrow-Leaved Dock
Buttercup Family
    Water Crowfoot
      (Water Buttercup)
    Baneberry
    Canada Anemone
    Western Clematis
    Wind Flower
Carrot Family
    Cow Parsnip
    Water Hemlock
Cattail Family
    Common Cattail
Composite Family
    Arrow-Leaved Sweet Coltsfoot
    Ox-Eye Daisy
    Pineapple Weed
    Tufted Fleabane
    Yarrow
Currant Family
    Northern Gooseberry
Dogbane Family
    Spreading Dogbane
Dogwood Family
    Bunchberry (Dwarf Dogwood)
    Red Osier Dogwood
Evening Primrose Family
    Gumbo Evening-Primrose
      (Butte-Primrose)
Ginseng Family
    Wild Sarsaparilla
Grass-of-Parnassus Family
    Grass-of-Parnassus

Heath Family
    Blueberry (Canada Blueberry)
    Bog Cranberry
    Greenish-Flowered Wintergreen
    Indian-Pipe (Ghost Plant)
    Labrador Tea
    One-Sided Wintergreen
    Single Delight
Honeysuckle Family
    Low-Bush Cranberry
      (Mooseberry)
    Snowberry
    Twinflower
Lily Family
    Carrion Flower
    Death Camas
    Fairybells
    False Solomon's-Seal
    Prairie Onion
    White Camas
Madder Family
    Northern Bedstraw
    Sweet-Scented Bedstraw
Milkwort Family
    Seneca Snakeroot
Morning Glory Family
    Morning Glory
Mustard Family
    Pennycress (Stinkweed)
Nightshade Family
    Black Henbane
Orchid Family
    Hooded Ladies' Tresses
    Round-Leaved Orchid
    Sparrow's-Egg Lady's Slipper
      (Franklin's Lady's Slipper)
Pea Family
    Ground-Plum
    White Clover (Dutch Clover)
    White Peavine
    Wild Licorice
Phlox Family
    Moss Phlox

Pink Family
    Field Chickweed
      (Mouse-Ear Chickweed)
    Night-Flowering Catchfly
Primrose Family
    Mealy Primrose
Purslane Family
    Western Spring Beauty
Rose Family
    Birch-Leaf Spirea
    Black Hawthorn
    Chokecherry
    Pin Cherry
    Saskatoon (Serviceberry)
    Trailing Raspberry
    White Cinquefoil
    Wild Red Raspberry
    Wild Strawberry
Sandalwood Family
    Pale Comandra
      (Bastard Toadflax)
Saxifrage Family
    Richardson's Alumroot
Violet Family
    Western Canada Violet
Water Plantain Family
    Arrowhead (Wapato)

YELLOW FLOWERS

Bladderwort Family
    Common Bladderwort
Borage Family
    Puccoon (Lemonweed)
    Western False Gromwell
Broom-Rape Family
    Clustered Broom-Rape
Buckwheat Family
    Yellow Buckwheat
      (Umbrella Plant)
Buttercup Family
    Creeping Buttercup
      (Seaside Buttercup)
    Marsh-Marigold
    Meadow Buttercup

Cactus Family
   Prickly-Pear Cactus
Carrot Family
   Heart-Leaved Alexanders
      (Meadow Parsnip)
   Leafy Musineon
   Snakeroot
Composite Family
   Annual Hawk's-Beard
   Arrow-Leaved Balsamroot
   Black-Eyed Susan
   Broomweed (Snakeweed)
   Brown-Eyed Susan
   Colorado Rubber Weed
   Common Tansy
   Dandelion
   Goat's-Beard
   Gumweed
   Hairy Golden Aster
   Heart-Leaved Arnica
   Late Goldenrod
   Marsh Ragwort
   Narrow-Leaved Hawkweed
   Nodding Beggarticks
   Perennial Sow-Thistle
   Prairie Coneflower
   Prairie Groundsel
      (Woolly Groundsel)
   Prairie Sunflower
   Shining Arnica (Orange Arnica)
   Short-Beaked Agoseris
      (False Dandelion)
   Sneezeweed
   Stemless Rubber Weed
      (Butte Marigold)
Evening Primrose Family
   Yellow Evening-Primrose
Figwort Family
   Butter and Eggs
   Common Mullein
   Yellow Beardtongue
   Yellow Monkeyflower

Fumitory Family
   Golden Corydalis
Honeysuckle Family
   Twining Honeysuckle
Lily Family
   Yellowbell
Mustard Family
   Prairie Rocket
   Sand Bladderpod
Oleaster Family
   Soopolallie
      (Canadian Buffaloberry)
   Wolf Willow (Silverberry)
Orchid Family
   Yellow Lady's Slipper
Pea Family
   Buffalo Bean (Golden Bean)
   Caragana
   Cushion Milk-Vetch
   Field Locoweed
   Yellow Hedysarum
   Yellow Sweet-Clover
Primrose Family
   Fringed Loosestrife
Rose Family
   Agrimony
   Early Cinquefoil
   Shrubby Cinquefoil
   Silverweed
Stonecrop Family
   Narrow-Petaled Stonecrop
Touch-Me-Not Family
   Jewelweed (Touch-Me-Not)
Violet Family
   Yellow Prairie Violet
Water Lily Family
   Yellow Pond Lily
      (Yellow Water Lily)

PHOTOGRAPH CREDITS

All photographs are by the author except those listed below, with sincere thanks by the author to the photographers for their gracious permission to use their work in this book.

Lorna Allen
Alpine Harebell page 21
Jones' Columbine page 4
Mist Maiden page 116
Partridgefoot page 99
Smooth Alpine Gentian page 19

Anne Elliott
Alpine Bistort page 37
Common Stonecrop page 153
Dwarf Raspberry page 192

Dennis Hall
River Beauty page 165

Glen Lee
Bog Cranberry page 171

Gill Ross
Beargrass page 70
Mountain Marsh Marigold page 41

Western St. John's Wort page 152
White Section Start page 34
Yellow Mountain Saxifrage page 151

Cliff Wallis
Green Saxifrage page 110
Kittentails page 14
Mountain Gentian page 17
Purple Saxifrage page 32

Russ Webb
Jacob's Ladder page 29

Cleve Wershler
Alpine Hawk's-Beard page 124
Alpine Wallflower page 186
Dwarf Sawwort page 7

Alan Youell
Alpine Poppy page 146

BIBLIOGRAPHY

Clark, L.J. and J. Trelawny (eds.), 1973, 1976, 1998. *Wildflowers of the Pacific Northwest.* Harbour Publishing, Madeira Park, British Columbia.

Cormack, R.G.H., 1977. *Wild Flowers of Alberta.* Hurtig Publishers, Edmonton, Alberta.

Kershaw, L., A. MacKinnon and J. Polar, 1998. *Plants of the Rocky Mountains.* Lone Pine Publishing, Edmonton, Alberta.

Parish, R., R. Coupe and D. Lloyd (eds.), 1996. *Plants of Southern Interior British Columbia.* Lone Pine Publishing, Edmonton, Alberta. ll

Phillips, W. H., 2001. *Northern Rocky Mountain Wildflowers.* Falcon, Helena, Montana.

Scotter, G. W., H. Flygare, 1986. *Wildflowers of the Canadian Rockies.* Hurtig Publishers Ltd., Toronto, Ontario.

Vance, F. R., J. R. Jowsey and J. S. McLean, 1977. *Wildflowers Across the Prairies.* Western Producer Prairie Books, Saskatoon, Saskatchewan.

Wilkinson, K., 1999. *Wildflowers of Alberta.* The University of Alberta Press and Lone Pine Publishing, Edmonton, Alberta.

Appendix

There are two plant families that are well represented in this book that probably deserve some special attention—the Composite Family and the Pea Family.

The Composite Family (also known as Sunflower Family) is a very large plant family. In fact, it is one of the largest plant families, with over 20,000 species worldwide. Some are annuals, some are biennials, and some are perennials. Members of this family have flower heads that occur on the broadened top of the stem. Each flower head is composed of ray flowers (ray florets) and/or disk flowers (disk florets), attached to a common base, which is called a receptacle. Some species have both ray and disk flowers; some have ray flowers only; and some have disk flowers only. Ray flowers are generally strap-like, and disk flowers are tubular and five-lobed at the tip. Attached to the rim and surrounding the flower head is a series of scale or leaf-like bracts, which is called the involucre. These bracts may be sticky glandular, or they may have spines. The fruits of Composites are single seeds called achenes, which often have a pappus—a cluster of hairs, bristles, or scales— at the top. The pappus may assist in seed dispersal, by wind or by attachment to passing humans and animals.

Some groups in the Composite Family can be difficult to identify. Perhaps the best example of that difficulty is seen in the Fleabanes and the Asters. Fleabanes are often referred to as Daisies. Fleabanes usually flower earlier than do Asters, but blooming times can overlap. Fleabanes are usually shorter and have fewer leaves and flowers than Asters. Fleabanes tend to have more and narrower ray flowers than Asters. The best way to determine whether you are dealing with a Fleabane or an Aster, however, is to closely examine the involucral bracts of the specimen—even resorting to some magnification. The bracts in Fleabanes are arranged in a single row and are usually equal in length. The bracts in Asters occur in several rows, are stiffer and thicker, often display a white base and green tips, and overlap like shingles.

The Pea Family (also known as Legumes) is also a very large plant family, with about 14,000 species worldwide. Many of these are cultivated species, and have been food sources for thousands of years. Members of the Pea Family are most easily recognized by their flowers, which have a very distinctive shape. The flowers are composed of 5 highly differentiated petals. The uppermost petal is called a standard (or banner). It is usually the largest and showiest petal. Below the standard are 2 side petals called wings. The 2 lowest petals are fused together, forming the keel. The keel typically encloses the 10 stamens, 9 of which are generally fused into a tube. The fruits of members of the Pea Family are enclosed in a characteristic seed pod known as a legume. Legumes split in 2 when mature, releasing the seeds into the environment. Most members of the Pea Family have compound leaves. Some are palmately compound, like the fingers on a hand. Lupines are a good example of such leaf construction. Other pea species have pinnately divided leaves, with leaflets arranged in opposite pairs along the stem. Some species have a modified leaf called a tendril, which allows the plant to attach itself to supports and thereby climb. Members of the Pea Family can contribute greatly to soil nutrients. They have nodules on their roots that contain nitrogen-fixing bacteria that convert atmospheric nitrogen into compounds the plant can utilize. In this way the soil is enriched.

INDEX

Photo by Dennis Hall

Neil Jennings is an ardent fly fisher, hiker, and photographer who loves "getting down in the dirt" to gaze at wildflowers. For twenty-two years he co-owned Country Pleasures, a fly fishing retailer in Calgary. He fly fishes extensively, both in fresh and salt water, and his angling pursuits usually lead him to wildflower investigations in a variety of venues. He has taught fly fishing courses in Calgary for over twenty years, and his photographs and writings on the subject have appeared in a number of outdoor magazines. Neil lives in Calgary with Linda, his wife of more than thirty years. They spend countless hours outdoors together, chasing fish, flowers, and – as often as possible – grandchildren.